Hard Press

Contents

CHAPTER I

ROOM NO. 317

I laid my papers down upon the broad mahogany counter, and exchanged greetings with the tall frock-coated reception clerk who came smiling towards me.

"I should like a single room on the third floor east, about the middle corridor," I said. "Can you manage that for me? 317 I had last time."

He shook his head at once. "I am very sorry, Mr. Courage," he said, "but all the rooms in that corridor are engaged. We will give you one on the second floor at the same price."

I was about to close with his offer, when, with a word of excuse, he hurried away to intercept some one who was passing through the hall. A junior clerk took his place, and consulted the plan for a moment doubtfully.

"There are several rooms exactly in the locality you asked for," he remarked, "which are simply being held over. If you would prefer 317, you can have it, and I will give 217 to our other client."

"Thank you," I answered, "I should prefer 317 if you can manage it."

He scribbled the number upon a ticket and handed it to the porter, who stood behind with my dressing-case. A page caught up the key, and I followed them to the lift. In the light of things which happened afterwards, I have sometimes wondered what became of the unfortunate junior clerk who gave me room number 317.

* * * * *

It was six o'clock when I arrived at the Hotel Universal. I washed, changed my clothes, and was shaved in the barber's shop. Afterwards, I spent, I think, the ordinary countryman's evening about town—having some regard always to the purpose of my visit. I dined at my club, went on to the Empire with a couple of friends, supped at the Savoy, and, after a brief return visit to the club, a single game of billiards and a final whisky and soda, returned to my hotel contented and sleepy, and quite prepared to tumble into bed. By some chance—the history of nations, as my own did, will sometimes turn upon such slight events—I left my door ajar whilst I sat upon the edge of the bed finishing a cigarette and treeing my boots, preparatory to depositing them outside. Suddenly my attention was arrested by a somewhat curious sound. I distinctly heard the swift, stealthy footsteps of a man running at full speed along the corridor. I leaned forward to listen. Then, without a moment's warning, they paused outside my door. It was hastily pushed open and as hastily closed. A man, half clothed and panting, was standing facing me—a strange, pitiable object. The boots slipped from my fingers. I stared at him in blank bewilderment.

"What the devil—" I began.

4

He made an anguished appeal to me for silence. Then I heard other footsteps in the corridor pausing outside my closed door. There was a moment's silence, then a soft muffled knocking. I moved towards it, only to be met by the intruder's frenzied whisper—

"For God's sake keep quiet!"

The man's hot breath scorched my cheek, his hands gripped my arm with nervous force, his hysterical whisper was barely audible, although his lips were within a few inches of my ear.

"Keep quiet," he muttered, "and don't open the door!"

"Why not?" I asked.

"They will kill me," he answered simply.

I resumed my seat on the side of the bed. My sensations were a little confused. Under ordinary circumstances, I should probably have been angry. It was impossible, however, to persevere in such a sentiment towards the abject creature who cowered by my side.

Yet, after all, was he abject? I looked away from the door, and, for the second time, studied carefully the features of the man who had sought my protection in so extraordinary a manner. He was clean shaven, his features were good; his face, under ordinary circumstances, might have been described as almost prepossessing. Just now it was whitened and distorted by fear to such an extent that it gave to his expression a perfectly repulsive cast. It was as though he looked beyond death and saw things, however dimly, more terrible than human understanding can fitly grapple with. There were subtleties of horror in his glassy eyes, in his drawn and haggard features.

Nothing, perhaps, could more completely illustrate the effect his words and appearance had upon me than the fact that I accepted his extraordinary statement without any instinct of disbelief! Here was I, an Englishman of sound nerves, of average courage, and certainly untroubled with any superabundance of imagination, domiciled in a perfectly well-known, if somewhat cosmopolitan, London hotel, and yet willing to believe, on the statement of a person whom I had never seen before in my life, that, within a few yards of me, were unseen men bent upon murder.

From outside I heard a warning chink of metal, and, acting upon impulse, I stepped forward and slipped the bolt of my door. Immediately afterwards a key was softly inserted in the lock and turned. The door strained against the bolt from some invisible pressure. Then there came the sound of retreating footsteps. We heard the door of the next room opened and closed. A moment later the handle of the communicating door was tried. I had, however, bolted it before I commenced to undress.

"What the mischief are you about?" I cried angrily. "Can't you leave my room alone?"

No answer; but the panels of the communicating door were bent inwards until it seemed as though they must burst. I crossed the room to where my portmanteau stood upon a luggage-rack, and took from it a small revolver. When I stood up with it in my hand, the effect upon my visitor was almost magical. He caught at my wrist and wrested it from my fingers. He grasped it almost lovingly.

"I can at least die now like a man," he muttered. "Thank Heaven for this!"

I sat down again upon the bed. I looked at the pillow and the unturned coverlet doubtfully. They had obviously not been disturbed. I glanced at my watch! it was barely two o'clock. I had not even been to bed. I could not possibly be dreaming! The door was straining now almost to bursting. I began to be annoyed.

"What the devil are you doing there?" I called out.

Again there was no answer, but a long crack had appeared on the panel. My companion was standing up watching it. He grasped the revolver as one accustomed to the use of such things. Once more I took note of him.

I saw now that he was younger than I had imagined, and a trifle taller. The ghastly pallor, which extended even to his lips, was unabated, but his first paroxysm of fear seemed, at any rate, to have become lessened. He looked now like a man at bay indeed, but prepared to fight for his life. He had evidently been dressed for the evening, for his white tie was still hanging about his neck. Coat and waistcoat he had left behind in his flight, but his black trousers were well and fashionably cut, and his socks were of silk, with small colored clocks. The fingers were white and delicate, and his nails well cared for. There was one thing more, the most noticeable of all perhaps. Although his face was the face of a young man, his hair was as white as snow.

"Look here," I said to him, "can't you give me some explanation as to what all this means? You haven't been getting yourself into trouble, have you?"

"Trouble!" he repeated vaguely, with his eyes fixed upon the door.

"With the police!" I explained.

"No, these are not the police," he answered.

"I don't mind a row particularly," I continued, "but I like to know something about it. What do these people want with you?"

"My life!" he answered grimly.

"Why?"

"I cannot tell you!"

A sudden and ridiculously obvious idea struck me for the first time. A small electric bell and telephone instrument were by the side of the bed. I leaned over and pressed the knob with my finger. My companion half glanced towards me, and back again instantly towards the door.

"No use," he muttered, "they will not come!"

Whereupon a thoroughly British sentiment was aroused in me. Of the liberties which had been taken with my room, both by this man and by his pursuers, I scarcely thought, but that any one should presume to interfere with my rights as an hotel guest angered me! I kept my finger on the knob of the bell; I summoned chambermaid, waiter, valet and boots. It was all to no effect. No one came. The telephone remained silent. The door was on the point of yielding.

I abandoned my useless efforts, and turned towards the man whom I was sheltering.

"How many are there in the next room?" I asked.

"Two!"

"If I stand by you, will you obey me?"

He hesitated for a moment. Then he nodded.

"Yes!"

"Get behind the bed then, and give me the revolver."

He parted with it reluctantly. I took it into my hand, only just in time. The door at last had burst away from its hinges. With perfect self-possession I saw one of the two men who had been engaged in its demolition calmly lean it up against the wall. The other stared at me as though I had been a ghost.

CHAPTER II

A MIDNIGHT RAID

I could see at once that neither of the two men who confronted me had really believed that the room into which their victim had escaped was already occupied by any other person than the one of whom they were in pursuit. Their expression of surprise was altogether genuine. I myself was, perhaps, equally taken aback. Nothing in their appearance suggested in the least the midnight assassin! I turned towards the one who had leaned the door up against the wall, and addressed him.

"May I ask to what I am indebted for the pleasure of this unexpected visit?" I inquired.

The man took out a handkerchief and mopped his forehead. He was short and stout, with a bushy brown beard, and eyes which blinked at me in amazement from behind his gold-rimmed spectacles. He wore a grey tweed travelling suit, and brown boots. He had exactly the air of a prosperous middle-class tradesman from the provinces.

"I am afraid, sir," he said, "that we have made a mistake—in which case we shall owe you a thousand apologies. We are in search of a friend whom we certainly believed that we had seen enter your room."

Now all the time he was talking his eyes were never still. Every inch of my room that was visible they ransacked. His companion, too, was engaged in the same task. There were no traces of my visitor to be seen.

"You can make your apologies and explanations to the management in the morning," I answered grimly "Pardon me!"

I held out my arm across the threshold, and for the first time looked at the other man who had been on the point of entering. He was slight and somewhat sallow, with very high forehead and small deep-set eyes. He was dressed in ordinary evening clothes, the details of which, however, betrayed his status. He wore a heavy gold chain, a dinner coat, and a made-up white tie, with the ends tucked in under a roll collar. He appeared to be objectionable, but far from dangerous.

"You are still a trifle over-anxious respecting the interior of my room!" I remarked, pushing him gently back.

He spoke to me for the first time. He spoke slowly and formally, and his accent struck me as being a little foreign.

8

"Sir," he said, "you may not be aware that the person of whom we are in search is a dangerous, an exceedingly dangerous character. If he should be concealed in your room the consequences to yourself might be most serious."

"Thank you," I said, "I am quite capable of taking care of myself."

Both men were standing as close to me as I was disposed to permit. I fancied that they were looking me over, as though to make an estimate of the possible amount of resistance I might be able to offer should they be disposed to make a rush. The odds, if any, must have seemed to them somewhat in my favor, for I was taller by head and shoulders than either of them, and a life-long devotion to athletics had broadened my shoulders, and given me strength beyond the average. Besides, there was the revolver in my right hand, which I took occasion now to display. The shorter of the two men again addressed me.

"My dear sir," he said softly, "it is necessary that you should not misapprehend the situation. The person of whom we are in search is one whom we are pledged to find. We have no quarrel with you! Why embroil yourself in an affair with which you have no concern?"

"I am not seeking to do so," I answered. "It is you and your friend who are the aggressors. You have forced an entrance into my room in a most unwarrantable fashion. Your missing friend is nothing to me. I desire to be left in peace."

Even as I spoke the words, I knew that there was to be no peace for me that night, for, stealthy though their movements were, I saw something glisten in the right hands of both of them. The odds now assumed a somewhat different appearance. I drew back a pace, and stood prepared for what might happen. My *vis-à-vis* in the gold-rimmed spectacles addressed me again.

"Sir," he said, "we will not bandy words any longer. It is better that we understand one another. There is a man hidden in your room whom we mean to have. You will understand that we are serious, when I tell you that we have engaged every room in this corridor, and the wires of your telephone are cut. If you will permit us to come in and find him, I promise that nothing shall happen in your room, that you shall not be compromised in any way. If you refuse, I must warn you that you will become involved in a matter more serious than you have any idea of."

For answer, I discharged my revolver twice at the ceiling, hoping to arouse some one, either guests or servants, and fired again at the shoulder of the man whose leap towards me was like the spring of a wild-cat. Both rooms were suddenly plunged into darkness, the elder of the two men, stepping back for a moment, had turned out the electric lights. For a short space of time everything was chaos. My immediate assailant I flung away from me with ease; his companion, who tried to rush past me in the darkness, I struck with a random blow on the side of the head, so that he staggered back with a groan. I knew very well that neither of them had passed me, and yet I fancied, as I paused to take breath for a moment, that I heard stealthy footsteps behind, in the room which I had been defending. I called again for help, and groped about on the wall for the electric light switches. The footsteps ceased, a sudden cry rang out from somewhere behind the bed-curtains, a cry so full of horror, that I felt the blood run cold in my veins, and the sweat break out upon my forehead. I sought desperately for the little brass knobs of the switches, listening all the while for those footsteps. I heard nothing save a low, sickening groan, which followed upon the cry, but I felt, a moment later, the hot breath of a human being upon my neck. I sprang aside, barely in time to escape a blow obviously aimed at me with some weapon or other, which cut through the air with the soft, nervous swish of an elastic life-preserver. I knew that some one who sought my life was within a few feet of me, striving to make sure before the second blow was aimed. In my stockinged feet I crept along by the wall. I could hear no sound of movement anywhere near me, and yet I knew quite well that my hidden assailant was close at hand. Just then, I heard at last what I had been listening for so long and so eagerly, footsteps and a voice in the corridor outside. Somebody sprang past me in the darkness, and, for a second, amazement kept me motionless. The thing was impossible, or I could have sworn that my feet were brushed by the skirts of a woman's gown, and that a whiff of perfume—it was like the scent of dying violets—floated past me. Then the door of my room, from which I had withdrawn the bolt, was flung suddenly open, and almost simultaneously my fingers touched the knob of the electric light fittings. The whole place was flooded with light. I looked around, half dazed, but eager to see what had become of my assailants. Both rooms were empty, or apparently so. There was no sign or evidence of any other person there save myself. On the threshold of my own apartment was standing the night porter.

"Have you let them go by?" I called out. "Did you see them in the corridor?"

"Who, sir?" the porter asked stolidly.

"Two men who forced their way into my room—look at the door. One was short and stout and wore glasses, the other was taller and thin. They were here a few seconds ago. Unless they passed you, they are in one of the rooms now."

The man came inside, and looked around him.

"I can't see any one, sir! There wasn't a soul about outside."

"Then we had better look for them!" I exclaimed. "Be careful, for they are armed."

There was no one in the adjoining room. We had searched it thoroughly before I suddenly remembered the visitor who had been the innocent cause of these exciting moments.

"By Jove!" I exclaimed, "there's a wounded man by the side of my bed! I quite forgot him, I was so anxious to catch these blackguards."

10

The porter looked at me with distinct suspicion.

"A wounded man, sir?" he remarked. "Where?"

"On the other side of the bed," I answered. "It's the man all this row was about."

I hurried round to where I had left my terrified visitor hiding behind the bed-curtain. There was no one there. We looked under the bed, even in the wardrobes. It was obvious, when we had finished our search, that not a soul was in either of the rooms except our two selves. The porter looked at me, and I looked at the porter.

"It's a marvellous thing!" I declared.

"It is," the porter agreed.

"You can see for yourself that that door has been battered in," I remarked, pointing to it.

The fellow smiled in such a manner, that I should have liked to have kicked him.

"I can see that it has been battered in," he said. "Oh! yes! I can see that!"

"You perhaps don't believe my story?" I asked calmly.

"It isn't my place to believe or disbelieve it," he answered. "I certainly didn't meet any one outside—much less three people. I shall make my report to the manager in the morning, sir! Good night."

So I was left alone, and, extraordinary as it may seem, I was asleep in less than half an hour.

CHAPTER III

MISS VAN HOYT

I was awakened at about nine o'clock the next morning by a loud and persistent knocking at the door of my room. I sat up in bed and shouted,

"Come in!"

A waiter entered bearing a note, which he handed to me on a salver. I looked at him, around the room, which was still in some confusion, and down at the note, which was clearly addressed to me, J. Hardross Courage, Esq. Suddenly my eyes fell upon the smashed door, and I remembered at once the events of the previous night. I tore open the note. It was typewritten and brief:—

"The manager presents his compliments to Mr. Hardross Courage, and would be obliged if he will arrange to vacate his room by midday. The manager further regrets that he is unable to offer Mr. Courage any other accommodation."

"Tell the valet to let me have a bath in five minutes," I ordered, springing out of bed, "and bring me some tea. Look sharp!"

I was in a furious temper. The events of the night before, strange though they had been, left me comparatively unmoved. I was filled, however, with a thoroughly British indignation at the nature of this note. My room had been broken into in the middle of the night; I had narrowly escaped being myself the victim of a serious and murderous assault; and now I was calmly told to leave the hotel! I hastened downstairs and into the office.

"I wish to see the manager as soon as possible," I said to one of the reception clerks behind the counter.

"Certainly, sir, what name?" he asked; drawing a slip of paper towards him.

"Courage—" I told him, "Mr. Hardross Courage!"

The man's manner underwent a distinct change.

"I am sorry, sir," he said, "but Mr. Blumentein is engaged. Is there anything I can do?"

"No!" I answered him bluntly. "I want the manager, and no one else will do. If he cannot see me now I will wait. If he does not appear in a reasonable time, I shall go direct to Scotland Yard and lay certain information before the authorities there."

The clerk stared at me, and then smiled in a tolerant manner. He was short and dark, and wore glasses. His manner was pleasant enough, but he had the air of endeavoring to soothe a fractious child—which annoyed me.

"I will send a message down to Mr. Blumentein, sir," he said, "but he is very busy this morning."

He called a boy, but, after a moment's hesitation, he left the office himself. I lit a cigarette, and waited with as much patience as I could command. The people who passed in and out interested me very little. Suddenly, however, I gave a start and looked up quickly.

A woman had entered the reception-room, passing so close to me that her skirts almost brushed my feet. She was tall, quietly and elegantly dressed, and she was followed by a most correct looking maid, who carried a tiny Japanese spaniel. I did not see her face, although I knew by her carriage and figure that she must be young. That she was a person of importance it was easy to see by the attention which was at once paid her. Her interest for me, however, lay in none of these things. I had been conscious, as she had passed, of a whiff of faint, very delicate perfume—and with it, of a sudden, sharp recollection. It was a perfume which I had distinguished but once before in my life, and that only a few hours ago.

She gave her key in at the desk, received some letters, and turning round passed within a few feet of me. Perhaps she realized that I was watching her with more than ordinary attention, and her eyes fell for a moment carelessly upon mine. They were withdrawn at once, and she passed on with the slightest of frowns—just sufficient rebuke to the person who had forgotten himself so far as to stare at a woman in a public place. The maid, too, glanced towards me with a slight flash in her large black eyes, as though she, also, resented my impertinence, and the little Japanese spaniel yawned as he was carried past, and showed me a set of dazzling white teeth. I was in disgrace all round, because I had looked for a second too long into his mistress' deep blue eyes and pale, proud face. Nevertheless, I presumed even further. I changed my position, so that I could see her where she stood in the hall, talking to her maid.

Like a man who looks half unwillingly into the land of hidden things, knowing very well that his own doom or joy is there, if he has the wit to see and the strength to grasp it, so did I deliberately falsify the tenets and obligations of my order, and, standing half in the hall, half in the office, I stared at the lady and the maid and the spaniel. She was younger even than I had thought her, and I felt that there was something foreign in her appearance, although of what nationality she might be I could not determine. Her hair was of a shade between brown and golden, and, as she stood now, with her back to me, I could see that it was so thick and abundant that her maid's art had been barely sufficient to keep it within bounds. In the front it was parted in the middle, and came rather low down over her forehead. Now I could see her profile—the rather long neck, which the lace scarf about her shoulders seemed to leave a little more than usually bare; the soft and yet firm outline of features, delicate enough and yet full of character. Just then her maid said something which seemed to call her attention to me. She half turned her head and looked me full in the face. Her eyes seemed to narrow a little, as though she were short-sighted. Then she very slowly and very deliberately turned her back upon me, and continued talking to her maid. My cheeks were tanned enough, but I felt the color burn as I prepared to move away. At that moment the lift stopped just opposite to her, and Mr. Blumentein stepped out, followed by his dapper little clerk.

Mr. Blumentein was a man of less than medium height, with grey hair and beard, powerfully built and with a sleek, well-groomed appearance. Hat in hand, and with many bows and smiles, he addressed a few remarks to the lady, who answered him courteously, but with obvious condescension. Then he came on to me, and his manner was very different indeed. The dapper little clerk, who had pointed me out, slipped away.

"Mr. Courage?" he inquired; "you wished to speak to me."

I handed him the typewritten communication which I had received.

"I wish for some explanation of this," I said.

He glanced at it, and shrugged his shoulders. "I cannot permit such proceedings as took place last night in this hotel," he said. "I can find no trace of the two persons whom you described as having broken into your room, and I am not at all satisfied with the explanations which have been given."

"Indeed," I answered. "I can assure you that I find the situation equally unsatisfactory. I come here in the ordinary way as a casual guest. My room is broken into in the middle of the night. I myself am assaulted, and another man, a stranger to me, is nearly murdered. If any explanations or apologies are due at all, I consider that they are due to me."

Mr. Blumentein edged a little away.

"You should consider yourself exceedingly fortunate," he declared, "to be spared the inconvenience of a police inquiry. My directors dislike very much any publicity given to brawls of this sort in the hotel, or you might find yourself in a somewhat awkward position. I have nothing more to say about it."

He would have moved away, but I stood directly in front of him.

"It happens that I have," I said. "I am not a thief or an adventurer, and my bona-fides are easily established. I am a magistrate in two counties; Sir Gilbert Hardross, who is a patron of your restaurant, is my cousin, and I expect him here to call for me within half an hour. I am up in town to play for my County against the M.C.C. at Lord's; I am a person who is perfectly well known, and my word as to what

14

happened last night will be readily accepted. If you do not alter your tone at once, I shall take a cab to Scotland Yard, and insist upon a complete investigation into the affairs of last night."

There was no doubt as to the effect of my words upon Mr. Blumentein. He was seriously perturbed, and wholly unable to conceal it.

"You can prove what you say, Mr. Courage, I suppose?" he remarked hesitatingly.

"Absolutely!" I answered; "look in this week's *Graphic*. You will see a photograph of me in the Medchestershire Cricket Team. Come into my room, and I will show you as many letters and papers as you please. Do you know that gentleman?"

"Certainly!" Mr. Blumentein answered, bowing low. "Good morning, Sir Charles!"

A young man in a flannel suit and straw hat sauntered up to us. He nodded condescendingly to the hotel manager, and shook hands with me.

"How are you, Courage?" he said. "I'm coming down to Lord's this afternoon to see the match."

He passed on. Mr. Blumentein was distinctly nervous.

"Will you do me the favor to come down to my room for a moment, Mr. Courage?" he begged. "I should like to speak to you in private."

I followed him down into his office. He closed the door, and set his hat down upon the desk.

"I have caused the strictest inquiries to be made, and I have been unable to obtain the slightest trace either of the man whom you say took shelter in your room, or the two others you spoke of. Under those circumstances, you will understand that your story did not sound very probable."

"Perhaps not," I admitted; "but I don't know what your night-porter could have been about, if he really saw nothing of them. I can give you a detailed description of all three if you like."

"One moment," Mr. Blumentein said, taking up pen and paper. "Now, if you please!"

I described the three men to the best of my ability, and Mr. Blumentein took down carefully all that I said.

"I will have the fullest inquiries made," he promised, "and let you know the result. In the meantime, I trust that you will consider the letter I wrote you this morning unwritten. You will doubtless prefer to leave the hotel after what has happened, but another time, I trust that we may be honored by your patronage."

I hesitated for a moment. It was clear that the man wanted to get rid of me. For the first time, the idea of remaining in the hotel occurred to me.

"I will consider the matter," I answered. "In the meantime, I hope you will have inquiries made at once. The man who took refuge in my room was in a terrible state of fright, and from what I saw of the other two, I am afraid you may find this a more serious affair than you have any idea of. By the bye, one of the two told me that they had engaged every room in that corridor. You may be able to trace him by that."

Mr. Blumentein shrugged his shoulders.

"That statement, at any rate, was a false one," he said. "All the rooms in the vicinity of yours were occupied by regular customers."

Now, in all probability, if Mr. Blumentein had looked me in the face when he made this last statement, I should have left the hotel within half an hour or so for good, and the whole episode, so far as I was concerned, would have been ended. But I could not help noticing a somewhat unaccountable nervousness in the man's manner, and it flashed into my mind suddenly that he knew a good deal more than he meant to tell me. He was keeping something back. The more I watched him, the more I felt certain of it. I determined not to leave the hotel.

"Well," I said, "we will look upon the whole affair last night as a misunderstanding. I will keep on my room for to-night, at any rate. I shall be having some friends to dine in the restaurant."

The man's face expressed anything but pleasure.

"Just as you like, Mr. Courage," he said. "Of course, if, under the circumstances, you preferred to leave us, we should quite understand it!"

"I shall stay for to-night, at any rate," I answered. "I am only up for a day or two."

He walked with me to the door. I hesitated for a moment, and then asked him the question which had been in my mind for some time.

"By the bye, Mr. Blumentein," I said, "if it is a permissible question, may I ask the name of the young lady with whom you were talking in the hall just now—a young lady with a French maid and a Japanese spaniel?"

Mr. Blumentein was perceptibly paler. His eyes were full of suspicion, almost fear.

"Why do you ask me that?" he inquired sharply.

"Out of curiosity, I am afraid," I answered readily. "I am sorry if I have been indiscreet!"

The man made an effort to recover his composure. I could see, though, that, for some reason, my question had disquieted him.

"The lady's name is Miss Van Hoyt," he said slowly. "I believe that she is of a very well-known American family. She came here with excellent recommendations; but, beyond her name, I really know very little about her. Nothing more I can do for you, Mr. Courage?"

"Nothing at all, thank you," I answered, moving towards the door.

"They have just telephoned down to say that a gentleman has called for you—Sir Gilbert Hardross, I believe."

I nodded and glanced at the clock.

"Thanks!" I said, "I must hurry."

"I will reserve a table for you in the restaurant to-night, sir," Mr. Blumentein said, bowing me out.

"For three, at eight o'clock," I answered.

17

CHAPTER IV

A MATCH AT LORD'S

My cousin, Gilbert Hardross, was eight years older than I, and of intensely serious proclivities. He was, I believe, a very useful member of the House, and absolutely conscientious in the discharge of what he termed his duty to his constituents. We drove down together to Lord's, and knowing him to be a person almost entirely devoid of imagination, I forbore to make any mention of the events of the previous night. One question, however, I did ask him.

"What sort of an hotel is the Universal supposed to be, Gilbert? Rather a queer lot of people staying there, I thought."

My cousin implied by a gesture that he was not surprised.

"Very cosmopolitan indeed," he declared. "It is patronized chiefly, I believe, by a certain class of Americans and gentlemen of the sporting persuasion. The restaurant, of course, is good, and a few notabilities stay there now and then. I should have thought the Carlton would have suited you better."

I changed the subject.

"How are politics?" I asked.

He looked at me as though in reproach at the levity of my question.

"You read the papers, I suppose?" he remarked. "You know for yourself that we are passing through a very critical time. Never," he added, "since I have been in the House, have I known such a period of anxiety."

Considering that Gilbert represented a rural constituency, and that his party was not even in office, I felt inclined to smile. However, I took him seriously.

"Same old war scare, I suppose?" I remarked.

"It has been a 'scare' for a good many years," he replied seriously. "People seem inclined to forget that behind the shadow all the time there is the substance. I happen to know that there is a great deal of tension just now at the Foreign Office!"

"Things seem pretty much as they were six months ago," I remarked. "There is no definite cause for alarm, is there?"

"No definite cause, perhaps, that we know of," my cousin answered; "but there is no denying the fact that an extraordinary amount of apprehension exists in the best informed circles. As Lord Kestelen said to me yesterday, one seems to feel the thunder in the air."

I was thoughtful for a moment. Perhaps, after all, I was inclined to envy my cousin. My own life was a simple and wholesome one enough, but it was far removed indeed from the world of great happenings. Just then, I felt the first premonitions of dissatisfaction.

"I believe I'm sorry after all, that I didn't go in for a career of some sort," I remarked.

My cousin looked gratified. He accepted my regret as a tribute to his own larger place in the world.

"In some respects," he admitted, "it is regrettable. Yet you must remember that you are practically the head of the family. I have the title, but you have the estates and the money. You should find plenty to do!"

I nodded.

"Naturally! That isn't exactly what I meant, though. Here we are, and by Jove, I'm late!"

My cousin cared for cricket no more than for any other sports, but because he represented Medchestershire, he made a point of coming to see his County play. He took up a prominent position in the pavilion enclosure, and requested me to inform the local reporters, who had come up from Medchester, of his presence. I changed into my flannels quickly, and was just in time to go out into the field with the rest of the team.

The morning's cricket was not particularly exciting, and I had hard work to keep my thoughts fixed upon the game. Our bowling was knocked about rather severely, but wickets fell with reasonable frequency. It was just before luncheon time that the most surprising event of the day happened to me. The captain of the M.C.C., who had just made his fifty, drove a full pitch hard towards the boundary on the edge of which I was fielding. By fast sprinting, and a lot of luck, I brought off the catch, and, amidst the applause from the pavilion within a few feet of me, I heard my cousin's somewhat patronizing congratulations:—

"Fine catch, Jim! Very fine catch indeed!"

I glanced round, and stood for a moment upon the cinder-path as though turned to stone. My cousin, who had changed his seat, was smiling kindly upon me a few yards away, and by his side, talking to him, was a young lady with golden-brown hair, a French maid dressed in black, and a Japanese spaniel. Her eyes met mine without any shadow of recognition. She looked upon me from her raised seat, as though I were a performer in some comedy being played for her amusement, in which she found it hard, however, to take any real interest. I went back to my place in the field, without any clear idea of whether I was upon my head or my heels, and my fielding for the rest of the time was purely mechanical.

In about half an hour the luncheon bell rang. I made straight for my cousin's seat, and, to my intense relief, saw that neither of them had as yet quitted their places. Gilbert seemed somewhat surprised to see me!

"Well," he remarked, "you haven't done so badly after all. Five wickets for 120 isn't it? You ought to get them out by four o'clock."

He hesitated. I glanced towards his companion, and he had no alternative.

"Miss Van Hoyt," he said, "will you allow me to introduce my cousin, Mr. Hardross Courage?"

She bowed a little absently.

"Are you interested in cricket, Miss Van Hoyt?" I asked inanely.

"Not in the least," she answered. "I have a list somewhere—in my purse, I think—of English institutions which must be studied before one can understand your country-people. Cricket, I believe, is second on the list. Your cousin was kind enough to tell me about this match, and how to get here."

"We are staying at the same hotel, I think," I remarked.

"Very likely," she answered, "I am only in London for a short time. Is the cricket over for the day now?"

I hastened to explain the luncheon arrangements. She rose at once.

"Then we will go," she said, turning to her maid and addressing her in French. "Janette, we depart!"

The maid rose with suspicious alacrity. The spaniel yawned and looked at me out of the corner of his black eye. I believe that he recognized me.

"Dare I ask you to honor us by lunching with my cousin and myself here, Miss Van Hoyt?" I asked eagerly.

She smiled very slightly, but the curve of her lips was delightful.

"And see more cricket?" she asked. "No! I think not—many thanks all the same!"

20

"I will put you in a hansom," my cousin said, turning towards her and ignoring me.

She looked over her shoulder and nodded. The maid looked at me out of her great black eyes, as though daring me to follow them, and, was it my fancy, or did that little morsel of canine absurdity really show me its white teeth on purpose? Anyhow, they strolled away, and left me there. I waited for Gilbert.

He reappeared in about five minutes, with a hateful smirk upon his well-cut but somewhat pasty features. I laid my hand upon his arm.

"Where did you meet her, Gilbert?" I asked. "Who is she? Where does she come from? How long have you known her?"

"Gently, my dear fellow!" he answered calmly. "I met her at Lady Tredwell's about a fortnight ago. I really know very little about her, except that she seems a charming young lady."

"Where does she come from?" I asked—"what country, I mean? She speaks like a foreigner!"

"Oh! she's American, of course," he told me—"a young American lady of fortune, I believe."

"American," I repeated vaguely, "are you sure?"

"Perfectly!" he answered.

"Any relatives here?" I asked.

"None that I know of," he admitted.

"Any connection with the stage?"

"Certainly not! I told you that I met her at Lady Tredwell's."

We walked into the luncheon room in silence. Presently my cousin showed signs of irritation.

"What the mischief are you so glum about?" he asked.

I looked up.

"I am not glum," I answered. "I was just thinking that the Hotel Universal seemed rather a queer place for a young lady with a French maid, a Japanese spaniel, and—-no chaperon."

"You are an ass!" my cousin declared.

* * * * *

It was not until the evening that Gilbert unbent. When, however, he studied the menu of the dinner which I had ordered for his delectation, and learned that I had invited his particular friend, Lord Kestelen, to meet him, he invited me to descend below to the American bar and take a cocktail while we waited for our guest.

"By the bye, Jim," he remarked, slipping his arm through mine, "I thought that Miss Van Hoyt was particularly inquisitive about you this morning."

"In what way?" I asked, at once interested.

"She wanted to know what you did—how you spent your time. When I told her that you had no profession, that you did nothing except play cricket and polo, and hunt and shoot, she seemed most unaccountably surprised. She appeared almost incredulous when I told her that you seldom came to London, and still more seldom went abroad. I wonder what she had in her head?"

"I have no idea," I answered thoughtfully. "I suppose it was only ordinary curiosity. In America all the men do something."

"That must be so, no doubt," my cousin admitted, "but it didn't sound like it. I wonder whether we shall see her this evening?"

I did not wonder at all! It seemed to me that I knew!

CHAPTER V

ON THE TERRACE

It was not until after my guests had departed, and I had almost given up hope, that I caught sight of her. She was seated at a table in the writing-room, and was in the act of sealing a letter. She looked up as I entered, and, after a second's hesitation, bowed coldly. I summoned up all my pluck, however, and approached her.

"Good evening, Miss Van Hoyt!" I said.

"Good evening, Mr. Courage!" she answered, proceeding to stamp her envelope.

"Have you been to the theatre?" I asked.

"Not this evening," she replied; "I have been to a meeting."

"A meeting!" I repeated; "that sounds interesting!"

"I doubt whether you would have found it so," she answered dryly.

Her manner, without being absolutely repellent, was far from encouraging. I found myself in the embarrassing position of having nothing left to say. I gave up all attempt at conversational philandering.

"May I talk to you for a few minutes, Miss Van Hoyt?" I asked.

She raised her head and looked at me meditatively. Her eyes were the color of early violets, but they were also very serious and very steady. She appeared to be deliberately taking stock of me, but I could not flatter myself that there was anything of personal interest in her regard.

"Yes!" she answered at last, "for a few minutes. Not here though. Go through the drawing-room on to the terrace, and wait for me there. Don't go at once. Go downstairs and have a drink or something first."

I could see her looking through the glass doors, and divining her wishes, I turned away at once. Mr. Blumentein was standing there, looking upon us. His smile was almost ghastly in its attempted cordiality. He took off his hat as I passed, and we exchanged some commonplace remark. I went downstairs and strolled up and down. The minutes passed ridiculously slowly. I looked at my watch a dozen times. At last I decided that I had waited long enough. I ascended the stairs, and made my way through the drawing-room on to the terrace. The place was deserted, but I had scarcely walked to the farther end, before I heard the soft trailing of a woman's skirt close at hand. I looked up eagerly, and she stepped out from the drawing-room. For a moment she hesitated. I remained motionless. I could do nothing but look at her. She wore a black evening dress—net I think it was, with deep flounces of lace. Her neck and arms were dazzlingly white in the half light; her lips were a little parted as she stood and listened. Her whole expression was natural, almost childlike. Suddenly she dropped the curtain and came swiftly towards me.

"Well," she said softly, "now that I am here, what have you to say to me?"

I was horribly tempted to say things which must have sounded unutterably foolish. With an effort I restrained myself. I addressed her almost coldly.

"Miss Van Hoyt," I said, "I want to know whether you are the only woman in this hotel who uses—that perfume."

She took out her handkerchief. A little whiff of faint fragrance came floating out from its crumpled lace.

"You recognize it?"

"Yes!"

"So much the better!" she declared. "Let me tell you this at once. I have not come here to answer questions. I have come to ask them. Are you content?"

"I am content—so long as you are here," I murmured.

"The man whom you protected last night—whose life you probably saved—on your honor, was he a stranger to you?"

"On my honor he was," I answered gravely.

"You have never seen him before?"

"To my knowledge—no!"

"You have never spoken to him before?"

"Never!"

She drew a little sigh.

"Your defence of him then," she said, "was simply accidental?"

"Entirely!" I answered.

24

"Has he communicated with you since?"

"Not in any way," I assured her.

She drew a little away from me. Her eyes were still fixed eagerly upon my face.

"Are you inclined to believe in me—to believe what I say?" she asked.

"Absolutely," I answered.

"Then listen to me now," she said. "That man, never mind his name, is one of nature's criminals. He is a traitor, a renegade, a malefactor. He has sinned against every law, he has written his own death-warrant. He deserves to die, he will die! That is a certain thing. He would have been dead before now, but for me! Do you know why I have made them spare his life?"

"No!" I answered. "Who are they? and who is to be his executioner? Surely, if he is all that you say there are laws under whose ban he must have come. It is not safe to talk like this of life and death here. All those things are arranged nowadays in the courts."

She smiled at me scornfully.

"Never mind that," she said. "You speak now of things which you do not understand. I want to tell you why I would not let them kill him."

"Well?"

"It is because if he is killed the secret goes with him. Never mind how he came by it, or who he is. It is sufficient for you to know that he has it. Up to now, he has resisted even torture. You remember the color of his hair? It went like that in a night, but he held out. Now he knows that he is going to die, and he is seeking for some one to whom he may pass it on."

"What is this secret then?" I asked, perplexed.

"Don't be absurd," she answered. "If I knew it, should I be likely to tell it to you? I have an idea of the nature of it, of course. But that is not enough."

"But—who is he then?" I asked. "How came he to obtain possession of it?"

"Now you are asking questions," she reminded me. "Believe me, you are safer, very much safer knowing nothing. If I were your friend—"

25

She hesitated. All the time her eyes were fixed upon me. She seemed to be trying to read the thoughts which were passing through my brain.

"If you were my friend," I repeated—"well?"

"I would give you some excellent advice," she said slowly.

"I am ready to take it!" I declared.

"On trust?"

"I believe so," I answered. "At least, you might give me the chance." She sank down upon the settee at the extreme end of the terrace. There was little chance here of being overheard, as we had a clear view of the only approach.

"After all," she said, "I do not think that it would be worth while. You belong to a class which I do not understand—which I do not pretend to understand. The things which seemed reasonable to me would probably seem banal to you. I am sure that it would be useless!"

"But why?" I persisted. "You have said so much, you must say more. I insist!"

A little wearily she pushed back the masses of hair from her forehead. Her head rested for a moment upon her fingers. Her eyes deliberately sought mine.

"Let me warn you," she said; "I am not the sort of woman whom you know anything about. The usual things do not attract me; I have never been in love with a man. I hope that I never shall be. And yet I think that I find my way a little further into life than most of my sex."

"You have other interests," I murmured.

"I have! What they are it is not for you to know. I am only interested in your sex so far as they are useful to me. You, if you were a different sort of man, might be very useful to me."

"At least give me the chance," I begged.

She shook her head.

"This morning," she said, "it seemed to me that I saw in one moment an epitome of your life. I saw every nerve of your body strained, I saw you wound up to a great effort. It was to catch a ball! You succeeded, I believe."

I laughed a little awkwardly.

"Yes! I caught it!" I remarked. "Success is something after all, isn't it?"

"I suppose so," she admitted. "Afterwards I spoke to your cousin about you. He told me that you lived on your estates, that you played games well, that you shot birds and rabbits, and sent to prison drunken men and poachers. 'But about his life?' I asked. 'This is his life,' your cousin answered. 'He has never gone in for a career!'"

"I suppose," I said slowly, "that this seems to you a very unambitious sort of existence!"

"Existence!" she answered scornfully, "it does not seem like existence at all! Your joys are the joys of a highly trained animal; your sorrows and your passions and your disappointments—they are at best those of the yokel. What has life to do with games and sports? These things may have their place and their use, but to make them all in all! The men whom I have met are not like that!"

"I am sorry," I said. "You see the other things have not come my way!"

"You mean that you have not been out to seek them," she declared. "The pulse of the world beats only for those who care to feel it."

"Let us take it for granted, for a moment, that you are right," I said, "and that I am a convert. I am willing to abjure my sports and my quiet days for a plunge into the greater world. Who will be my guide? Which path shall I follow?"

"You are not in earnest," she murmured.

"Perhaps I am, perhaps not," I answered. "At any rate, there have been times when I have found life a tame thing. Such a feeling came to me two years ago, and I went to Africa to shoot lions."

She leaned towards me.

"You should hunt men, not lions," she whispered. "It is only the animal courage in you which keeps you cool when you face wild beasts. It is a different thing when you measure wits and strength with one of your own race!"

"Count me a willing listener and go on," I said. "If you can show me the way, I am willing to take it."

"Why not?" she said, half to herself. "You have strength, you have courage! Why shouldn't you come a little way into life?"

"If it is by your side," I began passionately.

She stopped me with a look.

"Please go away," she said firmly. "You only weary me! If it is to gain an opportunity of saying this sort of rubbish that you have induced me to take you seriously, I can only say that I am sorry I have wasted a second of my time upon you!"

"The two things are apart," I answered. "I will not allude to the one again. My interest in what you have said is genuine. I am waiting for your advice."

She rose slowly to her feet. She looked me in the eyes, but there was no shadow of kindness in their expression.

"If I were a man," she said—"if I were you, I would seek out the person whom you befriended—he goes by the name of Guest—and I would learn from him—the secret!"

"Where can I find him?" I asked eagerly. "He seems to have disappeared entirely."

Her voice sank to a whisper. Her breath fanned my cheek, so that I felt half mad with the desire to hold her in my arms, if only for a moment. I think that she must have seen the light flash in my eyes, but she ignored it altogether.

"Go to your room," she said, "and wait till a messenger comes to you."

CHAPTER VI

"Mr. Guest"

I had been alone for nearly an hour before there came a cautious tapping at my door, I opened it at once, and stared at my visitor in surprise. It was the man in the grey tweed suit, who had broken into my room the night before.

"You!" I exclaimed; "what the mischief are you doing here?"

"If you will permit me to enter," he said, "I shall be glad to explain."

He stepped past me into the room. I closed the door behind him.

"What do you want with me?" I asked.

My visitor regarded me thoughtfully through his gold-rimmed spectacles. I, too, was taking careful note of him. Any one more commonplace—with less of the bearing of a conspirator—it would be impossible to imagine. His features, his clothes, his bearing, were all ordinary. His face had not even the shrewdness of the successful business man. His brown beard was carefully trimmed, his figure was a little podgy, his manner undistinguished. I found it hard to associate him in my mind with such things as the woman whom I had left a few moments ago had spoken of.

"I understand," he said, "that you wish for an interview with your friend, Mr. Leslie Guest. His room happens to be close to mine. I shall be pleased to conduct you there!"

"You have seen Miss Van Hoyt then?" I exclaimed.

"I have just left her!" he answered.

I stared at him incredulously.

"Do you mean to tell me," I said, "that, after last night, you have dared to remain in the hotel—that you have a room here?"

My visitor smiled.

"But certainly," he said, "you are under some curious apprehension as to the events of last night. My friend and I are most harmless individuals. We only wanted a little business conversation with Mr. Guest, which he was foolish enough to try and avoid. That is all arranged, now, however!"

"Is it?" I answered curtly. "Then I am sorry for Mr. Guest!"

Again my visitor smiled—quite a harmless smile it was, as of pity for some unaccountably foolish person.

"You do not seem," he remarked, "if I may be pardoned for saying so, a very imaginative person, Mr. Courage, but you certainly have some strange ideas as to my friend and myself. Possibly Mr. Guest himself is responsible for them! A very excitable person at times!"

"You had better take me to him, if that is your errand," I said shortly. "This sort of conversation between you and me is rather a waste of time."

"Certainly!" he answered. "Will you follow me?"

We took the lift to the sixth floor, traversed an entire corridor, and then, mounting a short and narrow flight of stairs, we arrived at a passage with three or four doors on either side, and no exit at the further end. We seemed to be entirely cut off from the main portion of the hotel, and I noticed that there were no numbers on the doors of the rooms. A very tall and powerful-looking man came to the head of the stairs, on hearing our footsteps, and regarded us suspiciously. Directly he recognized my companion, however, he allowed us to pass.

"A nice quiet part of the hotel this," my guide remarked, glancing towards me.

"Very!" I answered dryly.

"A man might be hidden here very securely," he added.

"I can well believe it," I assented.

He knocked softly at the third door on the left. A woman's voice answered him. A moment later, the door was opened by a nurse in plain hospital dress.

"Good evening, nurse!" my companion said cheerfully. "This gentleman would like to see Mr. Guest! Is he awake?"

The nurse opened the door a little wider, which I took for an invitation to enter. She closed it softly behind me. My guide remained outside.

The room was a very small one, and furnished after the usual hotel fashion. The only light burning was a heavily-shaded electric lamp, placed by the bedside. The nurse raised it a little, and looked down upon the man who lay there motionless.

"He is asleep," she remarked. "It is time he took his medicine. I must wake him!"

She spoke with a pronounced foreign accent. Her fair hair and stolid features left me little doubt as to her nationality. I was conscious of a strong and instinctive dislike to her from the moment I heard her speak and watched her bending over the bed. I think that her face was one of the most unsympathetic which I had ever seen.

She poured some medicine into a glass, and turned on another electric light. Her patient woke at once. Directly he opened his eyes, he recognized me with a little start.

"You!" he exclaimed. "You!"

I sat down on the edge of the bed.

"You haven't forgotten me then?" I remarked. "I'm sorry you're queer! Nothing serious, I hope?"

He ignored my words. He was looking at me all the time, as though inclined to doubt the evidence of his senses.

"Who let you come—up here?" he asked in a whisper.

"I made inquiries about you, and got permission to come up," I answered. "How are you feeling this evening?"

"I don't understand why they let you come," he said uneasily. "Stoop down!"

The nurse came forward with a wineglass.

"Will you take your medicine, please?" she said.

"Presently," he answered, "put it down."

She glanced at the clock and held the glass out once more.

"It is past the time," she said.

"I have had two doses to-day," he answered. "Quite enough, I think. Set it down and go away, please. I want to talk with this gentleman."

"Talking is not good for you," she said, without moving. "Better take your medicine and go to sleep!"

He took the glass from her hand, and, with a glance at its contents which puzzled me, drank it off.

"Now will you go?" he asked, handing back the glass to her.

She dragged her chair to the bedside.

"If you will talk," she said stolidly, "I must watch that you do not excite yourself too much!"

He glanced meaningly at me.

"I have private matters to discuss!" he said.

"You are not well enough to talk of private matters, or anything else important," she declared. "You will excite yourself. You will bring on the fever. I remain here to watch. It is by the doctor's orders."

She sat down heavily within a few feet of us.

"You speak French?" Guest asked me.

I nodded.

"Fairly well!"

"Watch her! See whether she seems to understand. I want to speak of what she must not hear."

She half rose from her chair. So far as her features could express anything, they expressed disquietude.

"She does not understand," I said. "Go on!"

She bent over the bedside.

"You must not talk any more," she said. "It excites you! Your temperature is rising."

He ignored her altogether.

"Listen," he said to me, "why they have let you come here I cannot tell! You know that I am in prison—that I am not likely to leave here alive!"

"I don't think that it is so bad as that," I assured him.

"It is worse! I am likely to die without the chance of finishing—my work. Great things will die with me. God knows what will happen."

"You have a doctor and a hospital nurse," I remarked. "That doesn't look as though they meant you to die!"

"You don't know who I am, and you don't know who they are," he answered, dropping his voice almost to a whisper.

"I want a month, one more month, and I might cheat them yet!"

"I don't think that they mean you to die," I said. "They have an idea that you are in possession of some marvellous secret. They want to get possession of that first."

"They persevere," he murmured. "In Paris—but never mind. They know very well that that secret, if I die before I can finish my work, dies with me, or—"

The nurse, who had left us a few moments before, re-entered the room. She went straight to a chair at the further end of the apartment, and took up a book. Guest looked at me with a puzzled expression.

"Stranger still!" he said, "we are allowed to talk."

"It may be only for a moment," I reminded him.

"Or pass it on to a successor who will complete my work," he said slowly. "I fear that I shall not find him. The time is too short now."

"Have you no friends I could send for?" I asked.

"Not one!" he answered.

I looked at him curiously. A man does not often confess himself entirely friendless.

"I need a strong, brave man," he said slowly—"one who is not afraid of Death, one who has the courage to dare everything in a great cause!"

"A great cause!" I repeated. "They are few and far between nowadays."

He looked at me steadily.

"You are an Englishman!"

I laughed.

"Saxon to the backbone," I admitted.

"You would consider it a great cause to save your country from ruin, from absolute and complete ruin!"

"My imagination," I declared, "cannot conceive such a situation."

"A flock of geese once saved an empire," he said, "a child's little finger in the crack of the dam kept a whole city from destruction. One man may yet save this pig-headed country of ours from utter disaster. It may be you—it may be I!"

"You are also an Englishman!" I exclaimed.

"Perhaps!" he answered shortly. "Never mind what I am. Think! Think hard! By to-morrow you must decide! Are you content with your life? Does it satisfy you? You have everything else; have you ambition?"

"I am not sure," I answered slowly. "Remember that this is all new to me. I must think!"

He raised himself a little in the bed. At no time on this occasion had he presented to me the abject appearance of the previous night. His cheeks were perfectly colorless, and this pallor, together with his white hair, and the spotless bed-linen, gave to his face a somewhat ghastly cast, but his dark eyes were bright and piercing, his features composed and natural.

"Listen," he said, "they may try to kill me, but I have a will, too, and I say that I will not die till I have found a successor to carry on—to the end—what I have begun. Mind, it is no coward's game! It is a walk with death, hand in hand, all the way."

He raised suddenly a warning finger. There was a knock at the door. The nurse who answered it came to the bedside.

"The gentleman has stayed long enough," she announced. "He must go now!"

I rose and held out my hand. He held it between his for a moment, and his eyes sought mine.

"You will come—to-morrow?"

"I will come," I promised. "To-morrow evening."

CHAPTER VII

A TÊTE-À-TÊTE DINNER

At about nine o'clock the following morning a note was brought to my room addressed to me in a lady's handwriting. I tore it open at once. It was, as I bad expected, from Miss Van Hoyt.

"*Dear Mr. Courage,*—

"I should like to see you for a few minutes at twelve o'clock in the reading-room.

"Yours sincerely,

"*Adèle Van Hoyt.*"

I wrote a reply immediately:—

"*Dear miss Van Hoyt,*—

"I regret that I am engaged for the day, and have to leave the hotel in an hour. I shall return about seven o'clock. Could you not dine with me this evening, either in the hotel or elsewhere?

"Yours sincerely,

"J. *Hardross courage.*"

Over my breakfast I studied the handwriting of her note. It might indeed have served for an index to so much of her character as had become apparent to me. The crisp, clear formation of the letters, the bold curves and angular terminations, seemed to denote a personality free from all feminine weaknesses. I was reminded at once of the unfaltering gaze of her deep blue eyes, of the chill precision of her words and manner. I asked myself, then, why a character so free, apparently, from all the lovable traits of her sex, should have proved so attractive to me. I had known other beautiful women, I was not untravelled, and I had met women in Paris and Vienna who also possessed the more subtle charms of perfect toilet and manners, and were free from the somewhat hopeless obviousness of most of the women of our country. There was something beneath all that. At the moment, I could not tell what it was. I simply realized that, for the first time, a woman stood easily first in my life, that my whole outlook upon the world was undermined.

Just as I was leaving the hotel, I saw her maid coming down the hall with a note in her hand. I waited, and she accosted me.

"Monsieur Courage!"

"Yes!" I answered.

She gave me the note.

"There is no reply at present," she said, dropping her voice almost to a whisper. "Monsieur might open it in his cab."

She gave me a glance of warning, and I saw that the hall porter and one of his subordinates were somewhat unnecessarily near me. Then she glided away, and I drove off in my cab. Directly we had started, I tore open the envelope and read these few lines.

"*Dear Mr. Courage,*—

"I will dine with you to-night at the Café Français at eight o'clock. Please take a table upstairs. Do not ask for me again or send me any further message until we meet there.

"Yours sincerely,

"*Adèle Van Hoyt.*"

At Lord's I was compelled to spend half the day hanging about the pavilion, smoking a good many more cigarettes than I was accustomed to, and finding the cricket much less interesting than usual. My own innings fortunately kept me distracted for a little more than two hours, and the effort of it soothed my nerves and did me good all round. On my way back to the hotel, I determined to forget everything except that I was going to dine alone with the one companion I would have chosen first out of the whole world. In that frame of mind I bathed, changed my clothes, and made my way a little before the appointed time to the Café Français.

I found out my table, sent for some more flowers, and ordered the wine.
Then I descended to the hall just in time to meet my guest.

She wore nothing over her evening dress save a lace scarf, which she untwisted as we ascended the stairs. For some reason I fancied that she was not very well pleased with me. Her greeting was certainly cool.

"Is this your favorite restaurant?" I asked, as the head-waiter ushered us to our table.

"I have no favorite restaurant," she answered; "only to-night I felt in the humor for French cooking—and French service."

36

I fancied that there was some meaning in the latter part of her sentence; but at that time I did not understand. I had ordered the dinner carefully; and I was glad to see that, although she ate sparingly, she showed appreciation. Wine she scarcely touched.

"So you have been particularly engaged to-day," was almost her first remark.

"I was forced to go to Lord's," I reminded her. "A cricket match lasts three days."

"Three whole days!" she exclaimed, raising her eyebrows.

"Certainly! unless it is over before," I replied.

"And you mean to say that you are a prisoner there all that time—that you could not leave if you chose to?"

"I am afraid not," I answered. "Cricket is a serious thing in this country, you know. If you are chosen to play and commence in the match, you must go through with it. Surely you have met with something of the same sort of thing in the football matches in America!"

"I have never been interested in such things," she said. "I suppose that is why I have never realized their importance. I am afraid, Mr. Courage—"

"Well?"

She lifted her eyes to mine. What a color!—and what a depth. Then I knew, as though by inspiration, how it was that I found myself passing into bondage. Cold she might seem, and self-engrossed! It was because the right chord had never been struck. Some day another light should shine in those wonderful eyes. I saw her before me transformed, saw color in her still, marble cheeks, saw her lips drift into a softer curve, heard the tremor of passion in her quiet, languid tone.

"Do you know that you are staring at me?" she remarked, calmly.

I apologized profusely.

"It is a bad habit of mine," I assured her. "I was looking—beyond."

There was real interest then in her face. She leaned a little forward. Perhaps it was my fancy, but I thought that she seemed to regard me differently.

"How interesting!" she said. "Do you know I had not given you credit for much imagination. You must tell me what you saw!"

"Impossible!" I declared.

"Rubbish!" she answered, "nothing is impossible. Besides, I ask it,"

"I do not know you well enough," I declared, helping myself to an artichoke, "to be personal."

"The liberties you take in your thoughts," she answered, "I permit you to render into speech. It is the same thing."

"One's thoughts," I answered, "are too phantasmagorial. One cannot collect them into speech."

"You must try," she declared, "or I shall never, never dine with you again. Nothing is so interesting as to see yourself from another's point of view!"

"Is it understood," I asked, "that I am not held personally responsible for my thoughts—that if I try to clothe them with words, I am held free from offence?"

She considered for a moment.

"I suppose so," she said. "Yes! Go on."

I drank off my glass of wine, and waited until the waiter, who had been carving a Rouen duckling on a stand by the side of the table, had stepped back into the background.

"Very well!" I said. "I am thirty-three years old and a bachelor, well off, and I have never been a stay-at-home. I know something of society in Paris, in Vienna, in Rome, as well as London. I have always found women agreeable companions, and I have never avoided them. The sex, as a whole, has attracted me. From individual members of it I have happened to remain absolutely heart-whole."

"Marvellous," she murmured in gentle derision. "Please pass the toast. Thank you!"

"I have been compelled," I said, "to be egotistical. I must now become personal. I saw you for the first time in the hall at the Universal, the morning before yesterday. I encountered you the night before under extremely dubious circumstances. I spoke to you for the first time yesterday. I have met other women as beautiful, I have met many others who have been more gracious to me. These things do not seem to count. You have asked for truth, mind, and you are going to have it. As surely as we are sitting here together, I know that, from henceforth, for me there will be—there could be—no other woman in the world!"

38

She moved in her chair a little restlessly. Her eyes avoided mine. Her eyebrows had contracted a little, but I could not see that she was angry.

"What am I to think of such a declaration as that?" she asked quietly. "You are not a wizard. You have seen of me what I chose, and you have seen nothing which a man should find lovable, except my looks."

I smiled as I leaned a little forward.

"Don't do me an injustice," I begged. "You have brought me now to the very moment when I forgot myself, and prompted your question. Remember that one has always one's fancy. I looked at you to-night, and I thought that I saw another woman—or rather I thought that I saw the woman that you might be, that I would pray to make you. The other woman is there, I think. I only hope that it may be my good fortune to call her into life."

Her head was bent over her plate. She seemed to be listening to the music—or was there something there which she did not wish me to see? I could not tell. The waiter intervened with another course. When she spoke to me again, her tone was almost cold, but it troubled me very little. There was a softness in her eyes which she could not hide.

"It seems to me," she said, "that we have been very frivolous. I agreed to dine with you that we might speak together of this unfortunate person, Leslie Guest. You saw him last night?"

"Yes," I answered, "I saw him."

My tone had become grave, and my face overcast. She was watching me curiously.

"Well!"

"I am bothered," I admitted. "I don't quite know what I ought to do!"

"Explain!"

"It seemed to me," I said, "that the man was neither more nor less than a prisoner there in the hands of those who, for some reason or other, are his enemies."

"That," she admitted, "is fairly obvious; what of it?"

"Well," I said, "the most straightforward thing for me to do, I believe, would be to go to the nearest police-station and tell them all I know."

She laughed softly.

"What an Englishman you are!" she exclaimed. "The law, or a letter to the *Times*. These are your final resources, are they not? Well, in this case, let me assure you that neither would help you in the least."

"I am not so sure," I answered. "At any rate, I do not see the fun of letting him remain there, to be done to death by those mysterious enemies of his."

"Then why not take him away?" she asked quietly.

"Where to?" I asked.

"Your own home, if you are sufficiently interested in him!"

"Do you mean that?" I asked.

"I do! Listen! I have no pity for the man who calls himself Leslie Guest! Death he has deserved, and his fate, whomever might intervene, is absolutely inevitable. But I do not wish him to die—at present!"

"Why not?"

"You can imagine, I think. He has the secret."

"He does not seem to me," I remarked, "the sort of man likely to part with it."

"Not to me," she answered quickly, "not to those others. From us he would guard it with his life! With you it is different."

"I am not sure," I said slowly, "that I wish to become a sharer of such dangerous knowledge."

"You are afraid?" she asked coldly.

"I do not see what I have to gain by it," I admitted. "I am not curious, and the possession of it certainly seems to entail some inconvenience, if not danger."

Her lip curled a little. She nodded as though she quite understood my point of view.

"You have said enough," she declared; "I perceive that I was not mistaken! You are exactly the sort of man I thought you were from the first. It is better for you to return to your cricket and your sports. You are at home with them; in the great world you would soon be weary and lost. Call for your bill, please, and put me in a cab. I have a call to make before I return to the hotel"

"One moment more," I begged. "You have not altogether understood me! I have spoken from my own point of view only. I have no interest in the salvation of Leslie Guest, beyond an Englishman's natural desire to see fair play. I have no wish to be burdened with a secret which seems to spell life or death in capital letters. But show me where your interest lies, and I promise you that I will be zealous enough! Tell me what to do and I will do it. My time and my life are yours. Do what you will with them! Can I say more than that?"

She flashed a wonderful look at me across the table—such a look that my heart beat, and my pulses flowed to a strange, new music. Her tone was soft, almost caressing.

"You mean this?"

"Upon my honor I do!" I answered.

"Then take Leslie Guest with you back to your home in the country," she said. "Keep him with you, keep every one else away from him. In less than a week he will tell you his secret!"

"I will do it," I answered.

CHAPTER VIII

IN THE TOILS

"This," the nurse said, after a moment's somewhat awkward pause, "is the doctor—Dr. Kretznow!"

A tall, awkwardly built man, wearing heavy glasses, turned away from the bedside, and looked at me inquiringly.

"My name is Courage, doctor," I said; "I am an acquaintance of your patient's."

The doctor frowned on me as he picked up his hat.

"I have given no permission," he said, "for my patient to receive visitors."

"I trust that you don't consider him too ill," I answered. "I was hoping to hear that he was better!"

"He is doing well enough," the doctor declared, "if he is left alone. But," he added, in a lower tone, "he is a sick man—a very sick man."

I glanced towards the bedside, and was shocked at the deathly pallor of his face. His eyes were half closed. He had not the air of hearing anything that we said. I walked towards the door with the doctor.

"What is the matter with him, doctor?" I asked.

He glanced towards me suspiciously.

"I was told," he said, "that my patient was without friends here, or any one for whom he could send."

"I have only known him a very short time," I answered, "but I am interested in him. If I may be allowed to say so, I am perfectly willing to defray any charges—"

He stopped me impatiently.

"I am physician to the hotel," he said, "Mr. Blumentein arranges all that with me!"

"Then perhaps as I have told you I am interested in him, I can trespass so far upon your courtesy as to inquire into the nature of his ailment," I said.

"I am afraid," he said, "that as you are not a medical man, I could scarcely make you understand."

"There was—an accident, I think," I began.

"A trifle! Nothing at all," the doctor declared hastily. "The trouble is with his heart. You will excuse me! I have many calls to make this evening."

"Perhaps you would kindly give me your address," I said. "Dr. Mumford, the heart specialist, is an acquaintance of mine. You would not object to meet him in consultation?"

He looked at me for a moment fixedly.

"It is not at all necessary!" he declared. "If Mr. Blumentein is not satisfied with my conduct of the case, I will withdraw from it at once! Otherwise, I shall not tolerate any interference!"

He left me without another word. I returned to the bedside. As I approached, Guest deliberately opened one eye and then closed it again. I addressed him in French:

"How are you?"

"About as I am meant to be," he answered.

The nurse came over to the bedside.

"It is not well for the gentleman to talk to-night," she said. "The doctor has said that he must be quite quiet."

"I shall only stay a few minutes," I answered; "and I will be careful not to disturb him."

She stood quite still for a moment, looking sullenly at us. Then she turned away and left the room. Guest raised himself a little in the bed.

"She has gone to fetch one of my—guardians," he remarked grimly.

"I am going to take you away from here—down to my home in the country," I said. "Do you think you can stand the journey?"

"Whether I can or not makes no difference," he answered. "I shall never be allowed to leave this room alive."

The Britisher in me was touched.

"Rubbish," I answered, "if you talk like that, I shall go to Scotland Yard at once. I tell you frankly, I don't like your nurse. I don't like your doctor, I don't like their shutting you up in this lonely part of the hotel, and I can't understand the attitude of Mr. Blumentein at all. He must know what he is risking in attempting this sort of thing, in London of all places in the world."

He interrupted me impatiently.

"Don't talk about Scotland Yard," he said. "These people are not fools. They would have a perfect answer to any charge you might bring."

"You don't mean that you intend to lie here and be done to death?" I protested.

"Death for me is a certain thing," he answered. "I have been a doomed man for months. There was never a chance for me after I entered the portals of this hotel. I knew that; but I backed my luck. I thought that I might have had time to finish my work—to lay the match to the gunpowder."

"Listen," I said, "there is a lady—a young lady staying here, a Miss Van Hoyt."

"Well?"

"It was her suggestion that I should take you away with me!"

His eyes seemed to dilate as he stared at me.

"Say that again," he murmured.

I repeated my words. He raised himself a little in the bed.

"What do you know of her?" he asked.

"Not much," I answered. "She came to Lord's cricket ground. My cousin was with her. We have spoken about you."

"You know—"

"I know that she is or appears to be one of your—what shall I say—enemies."

"She is willing," he repeated, "for me to go away with you! Ah!"

A sudden understanding came into his face.

"Yes!" he declared hoarsely, "I think that I understand. Go back to her! Say that I consent. She—she is different to those others. She plays—the great game! Hush! I go to sleep!"

He closed his eyes. The door opened, and the nurse entered, followed by a man who bowed gravely to me. He was still wearing a grey tweed suit and a red tie; his eyes beamed upon me from behind his gold-rimmed spectacles.

"Ah!" he exclaimed softly, "so you have come to see your friend. It is very kind of you! I trust that you find him better."

I pointed to the nurse.

"Send her away," I said. "I want to talk to you!"

"We will talk with pleasure," the newcomer answered, "but why here? We shall disturb our friend. Come into my room, and we will drink a whisky and soda together."

"Thank you, no!" I answered dryly. "I will drink with you at the bar, or in the smoking-room if you like—not in your room."

He bowed.

"An admirable precaution, sir," he declared. "We will go to the smoking-room."

I glanced towards the bed. Guest was sleeping, or feigning sleep. My companion's eyes followed mine sympathetically.

"Poor fellow!" he exclaimed. "I am afraid that he is very ill!"

I opened the door and pushed him gently outside.

"We will go downstairs and have that talk," I said.

We found a quiet corner in the smoking-room, where there was a little recess partitioned off from the rest of the room. My companion drew a small card-case from his pocket.

"Permit me, Mr. Courage," he said, "to introduce myself. My name is Stanley, James Stanley, and I come from Liverpool. Waiter, two best Scotch whiskies, and a large Schweppe's soda."

"Mr. Stanley," I said, "I am glad to know a name by which I can call you, but this is going to be a straight talk between you and me; and I may as well tell you that I do not believe that your name is Stanley, or that you come from Liverpool!"

"Ah! It is immaterial," he declared softly.

"I want to speak to you," I said, "about the man Guest upstairs. It seems to me that there is a conspiracy going on against him in this hotel. I want you to understand that I am not prepared to stand quietly aside and see him done to death!"

My companion laughed softly. He took off his spectacles, and wiped them with a silk handkerchief.

"A conspiracy," he repeated, "in the Hotel Universal. My dear sir, you are letting your indignation run away with you! Consider for a moment what you are saying. The hotel is full of visitors from all parts of England. It is one of the largest and best known in London. Its reputation—"

"Oh! spare me all this rot," I interrupted rudely. "Let me remind you of what happened two nights ago, when you broke into my room in search of Guest."

"Ah!" he remarked, "that, no doubt, must have seemed an odd proceeding to you. But, in the first place, you must remember we had no idea that the room was occupied. We were very anxious to have an explanation with our friend, purely a business matter, and he had irritated us both by his persistent avoidance of it. We have had our little talk now, and the matter is over. My partner has already left, and I am returning to Liverpool myself to-morrow or the next day. I fear that you were misled by my language and manner on that unfortunate evening. I am sorry; but I must admit that I was over-excited."

"Very good," I said. "Then, perhaps, as you are so fluent with your explanations, you will tell me why Mr. Guest has been removed to a part of the hotel which I am quite sure that no one knows anything about, is being attended by a doctor of most unprepossessing appearance, and a nurse who treats him as a jailer would!"

Mr. Stanley's face beamed with good-humored mirth.

"You young men," he declared, "are so imaginative. Mr. Guest has simply been removed to the part of the hotel which is reserved for sick people. No one likes to know that they have anybody next door to them who is seriously ill. As for the doctor, he is a highly qualified practitioner, and visits the hotel every day . by arrangement with the manager; and the nurse was sent from the nearest nurses' home."

"You think, then," I continued, "that if I were to go to Scotland Yard, and tell them all that I know, that I should be making a fool of myself."

46

Mr. Stanley's eyes twinkled.

"Why not try it?" he suggested. "There is a detective always in attendance on the premises. Send for him now, and let us hear what he says."

"Very well, Mr. Stanley," I said, "your explanations all sound very reasonable. I am to take it, then, that if Mr. Guest desired to—say leave the hotel to-morrow, no one would make any objection!"

Mr. Stanley was almost distressed.

"Objection! My dear sir! Mr. Guest is his own master, is he not? He pays his own bill, and he leaves when he likes. At present, of course, he is not able to, but that is simply a matter of health."

"I am proposing," I said, "to take Mr. Guest away with me into the country to-morrow."

Mr. Stanley looked at me steadily. There was a subtle change in his face. I was watching him closely, and I saw the glint of his eyes behind his spectacles. I began to think I had been rash to lay my cards upon the table.

"I am afraid," he said gently, "that you are proposing what would be—certain death to Mr. Guest—in his present state of health."

"I am afraid," I replied, "that if I leave him here, it will also be—to certain death!"

Mr. Stanley called to the waiter.

"One small drink more, and I must go to bed," he said. "Up to a certain point, I agree with you. I believe that Leslie Guest is a dying man. Whether he stays here or goes makes little difference—very little difference indeed to me. Your health, Mr. Courage! A farewell drink this, I am afraid!"

I raised my tumbler to my lips, and nodded to him. Then I rose to my feet, but almost as I did so, I realized what had happened. The floor heaved up beneath my feet, my knees trembled, I felt the perspiration break out upon my forehead. Through the mist which was gathering in front of my eyes, I could see the half-curious, half-derisive glances of the other occupants of the room; and opposite, Mr. Stanley, his eyes blinking at me from behind his spectacles, his expression one of grieved concern. I leaned over toward him.

"You d——d scoundrel!" I exclaimed.

After that, my head fell forward upon my folded arms, and I remembered no more!

CHAPTER IX

AN UNEXPECTED VISITOR

I sat up in bed, heavy, unrefreshed, and with a splitting headache. The clock on the mantelpiece was striking three o'clock; from below I could hear the clatter of vehicles in the courtyard, and the distant roar of traffic from the streets beyond. Slowly I realized that it was three o'clock in the afternoon; the events of the night before re-formed themselves in my mind. I rang the bell for the valet and sprang out of bed.

"Why didn't you call me this morning?" I asked angrily.

"You gave no orders, sir," the man answered. "I have been in the room once or twice, but you were sleeping so soundly that I didn't like to disturb you."

I began tearing on my clothes.

"What sort of weather has it been?" I asked.

"Pouring rain since seven o'clock, sir!" the man answered. "No chance of play at Lord's, sir!"

"Thank Heaven!" I exclaimed fervently. "Order me a cup of tea, will you, and—stop a minute—take this note round to Miss Van Hoyt—367."

He returned in a few minutes with the tea; but he brought my note back again.

"Miss Van Hoyt left the hotel this morning, sir," he announced.

I turned round quickly.

"She is coming back, of course!" I exclaimed.

"The chambermaid thought not, sir," the man declared. "She has given up her room, at any rate. They would know for certain down in the office."

I finished the rest of my toilet in a hurry, and went straight to the reception bureau. I fancied that the clerk to whom I addressed myself eyed me queerly.

"Can you tell me if Miss Van Hoyt has left the hotel?" I asked.

"She left this morning, sir," he replied.

48

"Is there any message for me—Mr. Courage?" I asked.

He disappeared for a moment, but I fancied that his search was only perfunctory.

"Nothing at all for you, sir," he announced.

I concealed my surprise as well as I could.

"Will you send my card up and ascertain if I can see Mr. Leslie Guest?" I asked. "He is staying somewhere in the south wing."

"Mr. Leslie Guest left just before one o'clock, sir," the clerk answered.

"Left the hotel!" I repeated. "Why! He was in bed yesterday, and scarcely able to move."

The clerk shrugged his shoulders. He had the air of being a little tired of me.

"He was probably better to-day," he answered. "At any rate, he was well enough to travel."

"Is Mr. James Stanley, of Liverpool, in?" I asked.

"Mr. Stanley paid his bill and went away at eight o'clock this morning," the man answered, going back to his ledger.

"I must see the manager at once," I declared firmly.

The clerk called a page-boy.

"Take this gentleman's name down to Mr. Blumentein," he ordered shortly.

I waited for several minutes. Then the boy returned, and beckoned me to follow him.

"Mr. Blumentein will see you in his office, sir," he announced. "Will you come this way?"

It was a very different Mr. Blumentein who looked up now, as I was shown into his private room. He regarded me with a frown, and his manner was indubitably hostile.

"You wish to speak to me, sir?" he asked curtly.

"I do!" I answered. "There is a good deal going on in your hotel which I do not understand; and I may as well tell you that I am determined to get to the bottom of it. I was drugged in the public smoking-room last night by a man who called himself Stanley, acting in collusion with one of the waiters."

Mr. Blumentein looked at me superciliously.

"Mr. Courage," he said, "the events of last night preclude my taking you seriously any more; but I should like you to understand that you have proved yourself an extremely troublesome guest here."

"What do you mean by the events of last night?" I asked.

"You were drunk in the smoking-room," Mr. Blumentein replied curtly, "and had to be assisted to your room. Don't trouble to deny it. There are a dozen witnesses, if necessary. I shall require you to leave the hotel within the next few hours."

"You know very well that I was nothing of the sort," I answered hotly.

"It is easily proved," Mr. Blumentein asserted. "Please understand that I am not prepared to discuss the matter with you."

"Very well," I answered. "Let it go at that. Whilst I was safely put out of the way, several of your guests seem to have left. Will you give me Miss Van Hoyt's address?"

"I will not," the manager answered.

"Mr. Leslie Guest's then?"

"I do not know it," he declared.

I turned towards the door.

"Very well, Mr. Blumentein," I said; "but if you imagine that this matter is going to rest where it is, you are very much mistaken. I am going straight to a private detective's, who is also a friend of mine!"

"Then for Heaven's sake go to him!" Mr. Blumentein declared irritably. "We have nothing to conceal here! All that we desire is to be left alone by guests whose conduct about the place is discreditable. Good afternoon, Mr. Courage!"

I returned to my room and had my bag packed. Then I sat down to think. I reviewed the course of events carefully since the night before last. Try how I could, I found it absolutely impossible to arrive at any clear conclusion with regard to them. The whole thing was a phantasmagoria. The one person in whom I had believed, and at whose bidding I was willing to take a hand in this mysterious game, had disappeared without a word of explanation or farewell. There could be only one reasonable course of action for me to pursue, and that was to shrug my shoulders and go my way. I had my own life to live, and although its limitations might be a little obvious, it was yet a reasonable and sane sort of life. Of Adèle I refused resolutely to think. I knew very well that I should not be able to forget her. On the other hand, I was convinced now that she was simply making use of me. I would go back home and forget these two days. I would reckon them as belonging to some one else's life, not mine.

I paid my bill, left the hotel, and caught the five o'clock train from St. Pancras to Medchester. From there I had a ten-mile drive, and it was almost dusk when we turned off the main road into the private approach to Saxby Hall—my old home. Every yard of the land around, half meadow-land, half park, I knew almost by heart; every corner and chimney of the long irregular house was familiar to me. It all looked very peaceful as we drove up to the front; the blue smoke from the chimneys going straight up in a long, thin line; not a rustle of breeze or movement anywhere. Perkins, my butler, came out to the steps to meet me, and successfully concealed his surprise at my return two days before I was expected.

"Any news, Perkins?" I inquired, as he helped me off with my coat.

"Nothing in any way special, sir," Perkins replied. "The cricket team from Romney Court were over here yesterday, sir, for the day."

"Gave 'em a licking, I hope?" I remarked.

"We won by thirty runs, sir," Perkins informed me. "Johnson was bowling remarkably well, sir. He took seven wickets for fifteen!"

I nodded, and was passing on to my study. Perkins followed me.

"We got your first telegram early this morning, sir!" he remarked.

I stopped short.

"What telegram?" I asked.

"The one telling us to prepare for the gentleman, sir," Perkins explained. "We had to guess at the train; but we sent the brougham in for the twelve o'clock, and Johnson waited. We've given him the south room, sir, and I think that he's quite comfortable."

"What the devil are you talking about?" I asked.

It was Perkins' turn to stare, which he did for a moment blankly.

"The gentleman whose arrival you wired about, sir," he answered. "Mr. Guest, I believe his name is."

"Mr. Guest is here now?" I asked.

"Certainly, sir! In the south room, sir! He asked to be told directly you arrived, sir!"

I turned abruptly towards the staircase. I said not another word to Perkins, but made my way to the room which he had spoken of. I knocked at the door, and it was Guest's voice which bade me enter. It was Guest himself, who in a grey travelling suit, which made him look smaller and frailer than ever, lay stretched upon the sofa over by the great south windows!

CHAPTER X

He sat up at once, but he did not attempt to rise. His eyes watched me anxiously. My surprise seemed to trouble him.

"I am afraid—" he began hesitatingly.

"You need be afraid of nothing," I interrupted, going over and taking his hand. "Only how on earth did you get here?"

He looked around before replying. The old habits had not deserted him.

"Your friend, Miss Van Hoyt, arranged it," he said. "The others had another plan; but they were no match for her."

"But how did you come?" I asked. "You were not well enough to travel alone."

"She left me at Medchester station," he answered. "Your carriage brought me over here, and your servants have been most kind. But—but before I go to bed to-night, there are things which I must say to you. We must not sleep under the same roof until we have arrived at an understanding."

I looked at him with compassion. He had shaved recently, and his face, besides being altogether colorless, seemed very wan and pinched. His clothes seemed too big for him, his eyes were unnaturally clear and luminous.

"We will talk later on," I said, "if it is really necessary. Shall you feel well enough to come down and have dinner with me, or would you like something served up here?"

"I should like to come down," he answered, "if you will lend me your man to help me dress."

"Come as you are," I said. "We shall be alone!"

He smiled a little curiously.

"I should like to change," he declared. "A few hours of civilization, after all I have been through, will be rather a welcome experience."

"Very well," I told him, "I will send my man at once. There is just another thing which I should like to ask you. Have you any objection to seeing my doctor?"

"None whatever," he answered. "I think perhaps," he added, "that it would be advisable, in case anything should happen while I am here."

I laughed cheerfully.

"Come," I declared, "nothing of that sort is going to happen now. You are perfectly safe here, and this country air is going to do wonders for you."

He made no answer in words. His expression, however, plainly showed me what he thought. I did not pursue the subject.

"I will send a man round at once," I said, turning away. "We dine at eight."

My guest at dinner-time revealed traces of breeding and distinction which I had not previously observed in him. He was obviously a man of birth, and one who had mixed in the very best society of other capitals, save London alone. He ate very little, but he drank two glasses of my "Regents" Chambertin, with the air of a critic. He declined cigars, but he carried my cigarette box off with him into the study; and he accepted without hesitation some '47 brandy with his coffee. All the time, however, he had the air of a man with something on his mind, and we had scarcely been alone for a minute, before he brushed aside the slighter conversation which I was somewhat inclined to foster, and plunged into the great subject.

"Mr. Courage," he said, "I want to speak to you seriously." I nodded.

"Why don't you wait for a few days, until you have pulled up a little?" I suggested. "There is no hurry. You are perfectly safe down here."

He looked at me as one might look at a child.

"There is very urgent need for hurry," he asserted, "and apart from that, death waits for no man, and my feet are very near indeed to the borderland. There must be an understanding between us."

"As you will," I answered, "although I won't admit that you are as ill as you think you are!"

He smiled faintly.

"That," he said, "is because you do not know. Now listen. You have to make, within the next few minutes, a great decision. Very likely, after you have chosen, you will curse me all your days. It was a freak of fate which brought us together. But I must say this. You are the sort of man whom I would have chosen, if any measure of choice had fallen to my lot. And yet," he looked around, "I am almost

54

afraid to speak now that I have seen you in your home, now that I have realized something of what your life must be."

All the time, underneath the flow of his level words, there trembled the sub-note of a barely controlled emotion. The man's eyes were like fire. His cigarette had gone out. He lit another with restless, twitching fingers.

"Words, at any rate, can do me no harm," I said encouragingly. "Go on! I should like to hear what you have to say."

"Words," he exclaimed, "bring knowledge, and with knowledge comes all the majesty or the despair of life. One does not need to be a student of character to know that you are a contented man. You are well off. You have a beautiful home, you are a sportsman, your days are well-ordered, life itself slips easily by for you. You have none of the wanderer's discontent, none of the passionate heart longings of the man who has lifted even the corner of the veil to see what lies beyond. If I speak, all this may be changed to you. Why should I do it?"

His words stirred me. The eloquence of real conviction trembled in his tone. I felt some answering spark of excitement creep into my own blood.

"Let me hear what you have to say, at all events!" I exclaimed. "Don't take too much for granted. Mine has been a simple life, but there have been seasons when I would have changed it. I come of an adventurous race, though the times have curbed our spirits. It was my grandfather, Sir Hardross Courage, who was ambassador at Paris when Napoleon—"

"I know! I know!" he exclaimed. "Your grandfather! Good! And Nicholas Courage—what of him?"

"My uncle!" I answered. "You have heard of him in Teheran."

A spot of color burned in his pallid cheeks.

"I hesitate no longer," he cried. "These were great men; but I will show you the way to deeds which shall leave their memory pale. Listen! Did you ever hear of Wortley Foote?"

"The spy," I answered, "of course!"

He started as though he were stung even to death. His cheeks were flushed, and then as suddenly livid. He seemed to have grown smaller in his chair, to be shrinking away as though I had threatened him with a blow.

"I forgot," he muttered. "I forgot. Never mind. I am Wortley Foote. At least it has been my name for a time."

It was my turn to be astonished. I looked at him for a moment petrified. Was this indeed the man who had brought all Europe to the verge of war, who was held responsible for the greatest international complication of the century? Years had passed, but I remembered well that week of fierce excitement when the clash of arms rang through Europe, when three great fleets were mobilized, and the very earth seemed to reverberate with the footsteps of the gathering millions, moving always towards one spot. Disaster was averted by what seemed then to be a miracle; but no one ever doubted but that one man, and one man alone, was responsible for what might have been the most awful catastrophe of civilized times. And it was that man who sat in my study and watched me now, with ghastly face and passionately inquiring eyes. When he spoke, his voice sounded thin and cracked.

"I had forgotten," he said, "that I was speaking to one of the million. To you, mine must seem a name to shudder at. Yet listen to me. My life is finished. I have lied before now in great causes. No man in my position could have avoided it. To-day, I speak the truth. You must believe me! Do you hear?"

"Yes!" I answered, "I hear!"

"Death is my bedfellow," he continued. "Death is by my side like my own shadow. In straits like mine, the uses of chicanery are past. I come of a family of English gentlemen, even as you, Hardross Courage. We are of the same order, and I speak to you man to man, with the dew of death upon my lips. You will listen?"

"Yes!" I answered, "I will listen!"

"You will believe?"

"Yes!" I answered, "I will believe!"

He drew a breath of relief. A wonderful change lightened his face.

"Diplomacy demanded a victim," he said, "and I never flinched. Two men knew the truth, and they are dead. My scheme was a bold one. If it had succeeded, it would have meant an alliance with Germany, an absolute incontrovertible alliance and an imperishable peace. France and Russia would have been powerless—the balance of strength, of accessible strength, must always have been with us. Every German statesman of note was with me. The falsehood, the vilely egotistic ambition of one man, chock-full to the lips with personal jealousy, a madman posing as a genius, wrecked all my plans. My life's work went for nothing. We escaped disaster by a miracle and my name is written in the pages of history as a scheming spy—I who narrowly escaped the greatest diplomatic triumph of all ages. That is the epitome of my career. You believe me?"

56

"I must," I answered.

"I was reported to have committed suicide," he continued. "Nothing was ever farther from my thoughts."

I followed an ancient maxim. I sought safety in the shadow of the enemy. I went to Berlin."

"The man who foiled you—" I said slowly.

"You know who it was," he interrupted. "The man who believes that he hears voices from heaven, that by the side of his Divine wisdom his ministers are fools and children, crying for they know not what! I may not see it, but you most surely will see the pricking of the bubble of his reputation. His name may stand for little more than mine, when the book of fate is finally closed."

He was silent for a moment, and glanced towards the sideboard. I could see the perspiration standing out in little white beads upon his forehead; he had the air of a man utterly exhausted. I poured him out a glass of wine, and brought it over. He drank it slowly, and reached out his hand for a cigarette.

"Never mind these things," he said more quietly. "A man in my condition should avoid talking of his enemies. I lived for two years quietly in Berlin. I changed as much of my appearance as illness had left recognizable; and during all that time I lived the ordinary life of a German citizen of moderate means, without my identity being once suspected. I frequented the cafés, I made friends with people in official positions. At the end of that time, I commenced to shape my plans. You can imagine of what nature they were. You can imagine what it was that I desired. I wanted to catch my enemy tripping."

I looked across at him a little incredulously. This was a strange story which he was telling me, and I knew very well, from the growing excitement of his manner, that its culmination was to come.

"But how could you in Berlin, alone, hope to accomplish this?" I asked.

"I knew the ropes," he answered simply, "and I lived for nothing else. I saw him drive amongst his people every day, and I bowed with the rest, I who could have spat in his face, I who carried with me the secret of his miserable perfidy, who knew alone why his ministers regarded him as a spoilt and fretful child. But I waited. Gradually I wormed my way a little into the fringe of the German Secret Service. I took them scraps of information; but such scraps that they were always hungry for more. I posed as a Dutch South African. They even chaffed me about my hatred for England. All the time I progressed, until, by chance, I stumbled across one of the threads which led—to the great Secret!"

There was a discreet knocking at the door. We both turned impatiently around. A servant was just ushering in our village doctor.

"Dr. Rust, sir," he announced.

CHAPTER XI

A LEGACY OF DANGER

I was scarcely aware myself to what an extent my attention had been riveted upon this strange story of my guest's, until the interruption came. The entry of the cheerful little village doctor seemed to dissolve an atmosphere thick with sensation. I drew a long breath as I rose to my feet. There was a certain measure of relief in the escape from such high tension.

"Glad to see you, doctor," I said mechanically. "My friend here, Mr. Guest, Dr. Rust," I added, completing the introduction, "is a little run down. I thought that I would like you to have a look at him."

The doctor sniffed the air disparagingly as he shook hands.

"Those beastly cigarettes," he remarked. "If you young men would only take to pipes!"

"Our insides aren't strong enough for your sort of tobacco, doctor," I answered. "I will leave you with Mr. Guest for a few minutes. You may like to overhaul him a little."

I made my way into the gardens, and stood for a few minutes looking out across the park. It was a still, hot evening; the scene was perhaps as peaceful a one as a man could conceive. The tall elms stood out like painted trees upon a painted sky, the only movement in the quiet pastoral landscape was where a little string of farm laborers were trudging homeward across the park, with their baskets over their shoulders. Beyond, the land sloped into a pleasant tree-encompassed hollow, and I could see the red-tiled roofs of the cottages, and the worn, grey spire of the village church. There was scarcely a breath of wind. Everything around me seemed to stand for peace. Many a night before I had stood here, smoking my pipe and drinking it all in—absolutely content with myself, my surroundings, and my life. And to-night I felt, with a certain measure of sadness, that it could never be the same again. A few yards behind me, in the room which I had just quitted, a man was looking death in the face; a man, the passionate, half-told fragments of whose life had kindled in me a whole world of new desires. These two, the man and the girl, enemies perhaps, speaking from the opposite poles of life, had made sad havoc with my well-ordered days. The excitement of his appeal was perhaps more directly potent; yet there was something far more subtle, far stranger, in my thoughts of her. She and her maid and her queer, black-eyed poodle were creatures of flesh and blood without a doubt; yet they had come into my life so strangely, and passed into so wonderful a place there, that I thought of them with something of the awe which belongs to things having in themselves some element of the mystic, if not of the supernatural. The blue of her eyes was not more wonderful than the flawless grace of her person and her environment. I could compare her only with visions one has read and dreamed about in the unreal worlds of poetry and romance. Her actual existence as a woman of the moment, a possible adventuress, certainly a very material and actual person, was hard indeed to realize.

I moved a little farther away into the gardens. The still air was full of the perfume of sweet-smelling flowers, of honeysuckle and roses, climbing about the maze of arches which sheltered the lower walks. To-night their sweetness seemed to mean new things to me. The twilight was falling rapidly; the shadows were blotting out the landscape. Out beyond there, beyond the boundaries of my walled garden, I seemed to be looking into a new and untravelled world. I knew very well that the old days were over. Already the change had come.

I turned my head at the sound of a footstep upon the gravel path. The doctor was standing beside me.

"Well," I asked, "what do you think of him?"

He answered me a little evasively. The cheerful optimism which had made him a very popular practitioner seemed for the moment to have deserted him.

"Your friend is in rather a curious state of health," he said slowly. "To tell you the truth, I scarcely know how to account for certain of his symptoms."

I smiled.

"He seems in a very weak state," I remarked supinely.

"Is he a very old friend?" the doctor asked.

"Why do you ask that?" I inquired curiously.

"Simply because I thought that you might know something of his disposition," the doctor answered. "Whether, for instance, he is the sort of man who would be likely to indulge in drugs."

I shook my head.

"I cannot tell," I said.

"There is something a little peculiar about his indifference," the doctor continued. "He answers my questions and submits to my examination, and all the time he has the air of a man who would say, 'I could tell you more about myself, if I would, than you could ever discover.' He has had a magnificent constitution in his time."

"Is he likely to die?" I asked.

60

"Not from any symptoms that I can discover," the doctor answered. "Yet, as I told you before, there are certain things about his condition which I do not understand. I should like to see him again in the morning! I am giving him a tonic, more as a matter of form. I scarcely think his system will respond to it!"

"It has not occurred to you, I suppose," I remarked, "that he might be suffering from poisoning?"

The doctor shook his head.

"There are no traces of anything of the sort," he declared. "My own impression is that he has been taking some sort of drug."

"Will you come in and have something?" I asked, as we neared the house.

The doctor shook his head.

"Not to-night," he answered; "I have another call to pay."

So I went back into the house alone, and found my guest waiting for me in some impatience. He was lying upon a sofa, piled up with cushions, and the extreme pallor of his face alarmed me.

"Give me some brandy and soda," he demanded. "Your village Aesculapius has been prodding me about, till I scarcely know where I am."

I hastened to the sideboard and attended to his wants.

"Well, did he invent a new disease for me?" he asked.

"No!" I answered. "On the contrary, he admitted that he was puzzled."

"Honest man! What did he suggest?"

"He asked whether you were in the habit of taking drugs," I answered.

"Never touched such a thing in my life," he declared.

"Neither did I," I remarked grimly, "until last night." And then I told him what had happened to me. He listened eagerly to my story.

"So there is a division in the camp," he murmured softly. "I imagined as much. As usual, it is the woman who plays the whole game."

"I wonder," I said, "whether you would mind telling me what you know of Miss Van Hoyt?"

He moved on the couch a little uneasily. The request, for some reason or other, seemed to disquiet him. Nevertheless, he answered me.

"Miss Van Hoyt," he said, "is an American young lady of excellent family and great fortune. She has lived for the last few years in Berlin and other European capitals. She has intimate friends, I believe, attached to the court at Berlin. She is a young person of an adventurous turn of mind, and she has, I believe, no particular love for England and English institutions."

"You number her," I remarked, "amongst your enemies?"

"And amongst yours," he answered dryly.

"Yet it was through her that I was able to bring you away," I remarked.

He turned his head towards me.

"You are not supposing, for one moment," he said, "that any measure of kindness was included in her motive."

"I suppose not," I answered doubtfully.

"Listen!" he said, "I fell into a trap at the Universal. I have been in danger too often not to recognize a hopeless position when I see one. I knew that escape for me was impossible. It was not as though my task were finished. I had months of work before me, and I was tracked down, so that I could not have moved except on sufferance. Our genial friend, whom you will remember in the grey tweed suit and glasses, and who has the knack of sticking to any one in whom he is interested like a leech, thought that my death, with as much dispatch as was wise, would be the simplest and pleasantest way out of the difficulty. The young lady, however, plays for the great stakes, She wanted to succeed where others have failed."

He paused for a moment, and drank from his tumbler. There were dark lines under his eyes, and I felt that I ought to stop him talking.

"Tell me the rest in the morning," I suggested. "I am sure that you ought to go to bed."

"You forget," he remarked grimly, "that for me there may be no morning. I am drawing very near the end, or even she would not have dared to let me come. Besides, you must understand, for it must be through you that she hopes—to succeed. She expects that I shall tell you, that you will be the legatee of this knowledge, which she would give so much to gain. And I suppose—don't be offended—that she counts you amongst the fools whom a woman's lips can tempt to any dishonor. You needn't glare at me like that. Miss Van Hoyt is very young and very beautiful. She has not yet learnt all the lessons of life—amongst which are her limitations. You see I do not ask you for any pledge—for any promise. But I do ask you, as an Englishman—and a man of honor—to take my burden from my back, and carry it on—to the end!"

I came over to his side.

"What does it mean?" I asked quietly.

"Death, very likely," he answered. "Danger always. No more sport, no more living in the easy places. But in the end glory—and afterwards peace. A man can die but once, Courage!"

"I am not afraid," I answered slowly. "But am I the man, do you think, for a task like this?"

"None better," he answered. "Listen, where do you sleep?"

"In the next room to yours," I answered.

"Good! Will you leave your door open, so that if I call in the night you may hear?"

"Certainly! You can have a servant sleep on the couch in your room, if you like."

He shook his head.

"I would rather not," he answered. "Just now I cannot talk any more. If my time comes in the night, I shall wake you. If not—to-morrow!"

CHAPTER XII

OLD FRIENDS

A flavor of unreality hung about the events of the last few days. I felt myself slowly waking as though from a nightmare. The dazzling sunshine was everywhere around us; the whir of reaping machines, the slighter humming of bees, and the song of birds, were in our ears; the perfume of all manner of flowers, and of the new-mown hay, made the air wonderfully sweet. My guest, in a cool grey flannel suit and a Panama hat, was by my side, looking like a man who has taken a new lease of life. He had patted my shire horses, and admired those of my hunters which were on view. He had walked three times round my walled garden, and amazed my head-gardener by his intimate acquaintance with the science of pruning. We had talked country talk and nothing else. From the moment when, somewhat to my surprise, he had appeared upon the terrace just as I was finishing my after-breakfast pipe, no word of any more serious subject had passed our lips. We had talked and passed the time very much as any other host and guest the first morning in a quiet country house. We were standing now upon a little knoll in the park, and I was pointing out my deer. He looked beyond to where the turrets and chimneys of a large, grey, stone house were half visible through the trees.

"Who is your neighbor?" he asked.

"Lord Dennisford," I answered. "A very decent fellow, too, although I don't see much of him. He spends most of his time abroad."

"Lord Dennisford!"

I turned to look at my companion. He had repeated the name very softly, yet with a peculiar intonation, which made me at once aware that the name was of interest to him.

"Yes! Do you know him?" I asked inanely.

"Is his wife here?" he asked.

"Lady Dennisford is seldom away," I answered. "She entertains a good deal down here. A very popular woman in the county."

He seemed to be measuring the distance across the park with his eyes.

"Let us go across and see her," he said.

I looked at him doubtfully.

"Can you walk as far?" I asked.

He nodded.

"Yes! I have my stick, and, if necessary, you can help me!"

So we set out across the park. I asked him no questions. He told me nothing. But when we had crossed the road, and were on our way up the avenue to Dennisford House, he clutched at my arm.

"I want to see her—alone," he muttered.

"I will see what I can do," I answered. "Lady Dennisford and I are old friends."

We reached the great sweep in front of the house. I pointed to the terrace, on which were several wicker chairs.

"The windows from the drawing-room, where I shall probably see Lady Dennisford, open out there," I remarked. "If you could give me any message which would interest her, perhaps—"

"Tell her," he muttered, "that you have a guest who walked with her once under the orange trees at Seville, and who—in a few days—will walk no more anywhere! She will come!"

He made his way along the terrace, leaning heavily upon his stick, and sank with a little sigh of relief into one of the cushion-laden wicker chairs. I watched him lean back with half-closed eyes; and I realized then what an effort this walk must have been to him. Before me the great front doors stood open, and with the familiarity of close neighborhood, I passed into the cool shaded hall, with its palms and flowers, its billiard-table invitingly uncovered, its tiny fountain playing in its marble basin. There was no one in sight; but, stretched upon a bright crimson cushion, set back in the heart of a great easy-chair, was a small Japanese spaniel.

Our recognition was mutual. The dog rose slowly to his haunches, and sat there looking at me. His apple-green bow had wandered to the side of his neck, and one ear was turned back. Yet notwithstanding the fact that his appearance was so far grotesque, I felt no inclinations whatever towards mirth. His coal-black eyes were fixed upon me steadfastly, his tiny wrinkled face seemed like the shrivelled and age-worn caricature of some Eastern magician. He showed no signs of pleasure or of welcome at my coming, nor did he share any of the bewilderment with which I gazed at him. But for the absurdity of the thing, I should have said that he had been sitting there waiting for me.

While I stood there dumfounded, not so much in wonder at this meeting with the dog, but amazed beyond measure at the things which his presence there seemed to indicate, he descended carefully from his chair, and crossing the smooth oak-laid floor, he made his way to the foot of the great staircase, and after a premonitory yawn, he indulged in one sharp penetrating bark. Almost immediately, the French maid came gliding down the stairs, still gowned in the sombrest black, still as pale as a woman could be. The dog looked at her and looked at me. Then, apparently conceiving that his duty was finished, he returned to his chair and curled himself up. I spoke to the maid.

"Is your mistress staying here?" I asked.

"But yes, monsieur!" she answered. "We arrived yesterday."

"Is she in now?" I asked. "Could I see her?"

"I will inquire," the maid answered. "Mademoiselle is in her room."

She turned and left me, and almost immediately the butler entered the hall. He was one of the local cricket eleven, and had been in service in the neighborhood all his life, so he knew me well, and greeted me at once with respectful interest.

"Is her Ladyship in, Murray?" I asked.

"I believe so, sir," he answered. "Will you come into the drawing-room?"

I followed him into Lady Dennisford's presence. She was writing letters in a small sanctum leading out of the drawing-room, and she looked round and nodded a cheery greeting to me.

"In one moment, Hardross," she exclaimed. "I've just finished."

I had known Lady Dennisford all my life; but I found myself studying her now with altogether a new interest. She was a slim, elegant woman, pale and perhaps a little insipid looking at ordinary times, but a famous and reckless rider to hounds, and an enthusiastic sportswoman. She was one of the few women concerning whom I never heard a single breath of scandal, notwithstanding her husband's long and frequent absences. She gave me little time, however, to revise my impressions of her; for, with a little spluttering of her pen, she finished her letter and came towards me.

"I hope you've come to lunch," she remarked; "I have the most delightful young person staying with me. You'll be charmed with her."

"A young lady?" I remarked.

"Yes! An American girl who talks English—and doesn't enthuse. Seems to know something about horses too!"

66

"Where did you discover this paragon?" I asked.

"My cousin sent her down. She knows everybody," Lady Dennisford answered. "I met her at lunch last week, and she spoke of hunting with the Pytchley next season. She's going to have a look at the country. Sorry the rain spoilt your match."

I hesitated a moment.

"Lady Dennisford," I said, "I had a particular reason for coming to see you this morning."

She raised her eyebrows.

"My dear Jim!"

"I, too, have a visitor," I told her; "rather a more mysterious person than yours seems to be. He is very ill indeed; and he is almost a stranger to me. But he was once, I believe, a friend of yours."

"A friend of mine!" she repeated. "How interesting! Do tell me his name!"

"I cannot do that," I answered, "because I do not know it—not his real name. But in the park this morning, I happened to tell him who lived here, and although he is very weak, he insisted upon paying you an immediate visit."

She looked around the room.

"But where is he?" she asked.

"He is outside on the terrace," I answered.

"My dear Jim!" she exclaimed, "really, all this mystery isn't like you. Aren't you overdoing it a little? Do call your friend in, and let me see who he is!"

"Lady Dennisford," I said, "of course, my guest may have misled me; but he seemed to think that an abrupt meeting might be undesirable. He wished me to tell you that he used once to walk with you under the orange trees of Seville, and to ask you to go out to him alone!"

Lady Dennisford sat quite still for several seconds. Her eyes were fixed upon me; but I am quite certain that I had passed from within the orbit of her vision. The things which she saw were of another world—somehow it seemed sacrilege on my part to dream of peering even into the dimmest corner of it. So I looked away, and I could never tell altogether what effect my words had had upon her. For when I looked up, she was gone! ...

CHAPTER XIII

THE SHADOW DEEPENS

"Mr. Courage!"

I looked up quickly. She was within a few feet of me, although I had not heard even the rustling of her gown. The dog, with his apple-green bow now put to rights, was sitting upon her shoulder. By the side of his uncanny features, it seemed to me that I had never sufficiently appreciated the fresh girlishness, the almost ingenuous beauty of her own face. She wore a plain, white, linen gown, and a magnificent blossom of scarlet geraniums in her bosom.

"Miss Van Hoyt!" I exclaimed.

She nodded, but glanced warningly at the window.

"They must not hear," she said softly. "Remember your cousin introduced you to me at Lord's—our only meeting."

My heart sank. I hated all this incomprehensible secrecy; a moment before she had seemed so different.

"Come out into the other room," she said. "They cannot hear us from there." We passed into the drawing-room. An uncomfortable thought struck me.

"You were here all the time!" I exclaimed.

"Certainly! I wanted to hear you and Lady Dennisford converse!"

"Eavesdropping, in fact," I remarked savagely.

"Precisely!" she agreed.

We were silent for a moment. Her eyes were full of mild amusement.

"I thought," she said demurely, "that you would be glad to see me."

"Glad! of course I am glad," I answered. "I'm such a poor fool that I can't help it. Why did you leave me in London without a word?"

"Why on earth not!" she exclaimed, smiling. "Besides, I knew that I should see you here very soon. I had to act quickly too! They did not want"—she glanced towards the terrace—"him to leave London."

"It was you, then," I remarked, "who had him sent down to my place?"

She nodded.

"It was not easy," she said. "If they had known that you were going to have a doctor to visit him, it would have been impossible."

"He has been poisoned, I suppose?" I said calmly.

She shrugged her shoulders.

"He will die, and die very soon," she answered. "That is certain. But I think you will find no doctor here who will have anything to say about poison."

She moved a little nearer to me. The overhanging bunch of scarlet geraniums from her waistband brushed against my coat; the beady black eyes of the dog upon her shoulder were fixed steadily upon me.

"Has he said anything?" she murmured.

"Not yet," I answered.

"He will do so," she declared confidently, "and before long. That is why I am here. You must come to me the moment—the very moment you know! You understand that?"

"Yes!" I answered, a little discontentedly, "I understand!"

Her expression suddenly changed. A frown darkened her face.

"Perhaps," she said, "you have already repented."

"Repented of what?" I asked quickly.

"That you have moved a little out of the rut, that you have taken a hand, even if it is a dummy's hand, in the game of life! Do you wish to draw back?"

"No!" I answered.

"Do you wish to be relieved of Leslie Guest? I could arrange it; it would be a matter of a few hours only."

"No!" I answered again. "I wish for one thing only!"

"And that?"

"You know!" I declared.

She turned a little way from me.

"I am not a magician," she declared.

"And yet you know," I answered. "A woman always does! I have no idea what these ties are, which seem to bind you to a life of mystery and double-dealing, but I should like to cut them loose. You have talked to me of ambition, of a larger life, where excitement and tragedy walk hand in hand! I should like to sweep all that away. I should like to convert you to my point of view."

She looked at me curiously. Never in my experience of her sex had I seen any one who varied so quickly in appearance, who seemed to pass with such effortless facility from the girl with the Madonna-like face and dreamy eyes, to the thoughtful and scheming woman of the world. Her rapid changes were a torture to me! I felt the elusiveness of her attitude.

"You would like me," she said scornfully, "to lead your village life, to watch the seasons pass from behind your windows. I was not born for that sort of thing! The thirst for life was in my veins from the nursery. You and I are as far apart as the North Star and the unknown land over which it watches! Sin itself would be less terrible to me than the indolence of such a life!"

"You have never tried it," I remarked.

"Nor shall I ever," she answered, "unless—"

"Unless what?"

She raised her eyebrows and flashed a sudden strange look upon me. There was mockery in it, subtlety, and a certain uneasiness which pleased me most. After all, she was like a beautiful wild young creature. The ways of her life were not yet wholly decreed.

"Unless the great magician comes and waves his wand," she declared. "The magic may fall upon my eyes, you know, and I may see new things."

I touched her hand for a moment. The dog's face was wrinkled like a monkey's, he growled, and his narrow red tongue shot out threateningly.

"It is that," I murmured, "which I shall pray for!"

70

She raised her head suddenly. We heard Lady Dennisford moving upon the terrace. She leaned over towards me.

"Leslie Guest," she whispered, "will not live for more than forty-eight hours. Make him tell you—to-night! To-morrow may be too late. Do you hear?—to-night!"

I was absolutely tongue-tied. Wherever else she failed, she was certainly a superb actress. A moment ago, she had been keeping my earnestness at bay with bantering words; then, at the sound of Lady Dennisford's approach, had come those few dramatic words; and now, at her entrance, I felt at once that I was the casual guest, being entertained as a matter of duty during my hostess' absence.

"I told you, didn't I, that I had met Mr. Courage in town?" she remarked, looking up. "After all, it is such a small world, isn't it?"

Lady Dennisford was scarcely in a condition to be observant. I believe that if we had been sitting hand in hand, she would scarcely have noticed the fact. She was very pale, and her eyes were exceedingly bright. She passed half-way through the room without even seeming to realize our presence. Then she stopped suddenly and addressed me.

"I am ordering a pony-cart," she said, "to take Mr. Guest back. He seems over-fatigued."

"Very thoughtful of you, Lady Dennisford," I answered. "We certainly did not mean to walk so far when we came out into the park."

A servant entered the room. She gave him some orders, and then, with a word of excuse to Adèle, she came over to my side.

"Hardross," she said softly, "what is the matter with him?"

"General breakdown," I answered; "I do not know of anything else."

"What does the doctor say?"

"The London doctor," I admitted, "gave little hope. Rust cannot discover that anything much is the matter with him."

"You yourself—what do you think?"

I hesitated. Her fingers gripped my arm.

"I think that he is very ill," I answered.

"Dying?"

"I should not be surprised."

She looked back towards the terrace. Her eyes were full of tears.

"Do what you can for him," she said softly. "He was once a great friend of mine. He was different then! Will you go out to him now? I promised to send you."

Guest was sitting upon the terrace, exactly as I had left him. His eyes were fixed upon vacancy, his lips were slightly curled in a meditative smile. There was a distinct change in his appearance. His expression was more peaceful, the slight restlessness had disappeared from his manner. But he had never looked to me more like a dying man.

"Lady Dennisford sent me out," I remarked, "She has ordered a pony-cart to take us home."

He nodded.

"I am quite ready," he said.

He tried to rise, but the effort seemed too much for him. I hastened to his aid, or I think that he would have fallen. He leaned on my arm heavily as we passed on our way to the avenue, where a carriage was already awaiting us.

"I was once," he remarked, in an ordinary conversational tone, "engaged to be married to Lady Dennisford."

"There was no—disagreement between you?" I asked.

"None that has not been healed," he answered softly.

"You would consider her to-day as a friend—not a likely enemy?" I asked.

He looked at me curiously.

"She is my friend," he answered softly. "Of that there is no doubt at all. Why do you ask?"

"Because," I answered, "for your friend, she has a strange guest."

"Whom do you mean?" he asked.

72

"Mademoiselle, and her maid—and poodle," I answered. "They are all here!"

I felt him shiver, for he was leaning heavily upon me. Nevertheless, he answered me with confidence.

"It is the gathering of the jackals," he muttered—"the jackals who are going to be disappointed. But you may be sure of one thing, my friend. The young lady is here as an ordinary guest! That was a matter very easy to arrange. There is a great social backing behind her. She can come and go where she pleases. But Lady Dennisford's knowledge of her is wholly innocent."

We drove back almost in silence. Rust was waiting for us when we arrived, and he eyed his patient curiously, and hurried him off to the house. They were alone together for some time, and when he came out his face was very grave. He came out into the garden in search of me!

"Courage," he said, "I wish to heavens I had never seen your guest!"

"What do you mean?" I asked. "Have you been quarrelling?"

"Quarrelling, no! One doesn't quarrel with a dying man," he answered.

"A dying man!" I repeated.

He nodded.

"He was on the verge of a collapse just now," he said. "I honestly fear that he will not live many more hours. Yet, though I could fill in his death certificate plausibly enough, if you were to ask me honestly to-day what was the matter with him, I could not tell you. Do you mind if I wire for a friend of mine to come down and see him?"

"By all means," I answered; "you mean a specialist, I suppose?"

"Yes!"

"On the heart?" I asked.

"No! a toxicologist!" Rust remarked dryly.

I glanced into his face. He was in deadly earnest.

"You believe—"

"What the devil is one to believe?" the doctor exclaimed irritably. "The man is sound, but he is dying. If I told you that I understood his symptoms, I should be a liar. I can think only of one thing. You yourself gave me the idea."

"Wire by all means," I said.

"I shall go to the village," Rust said, "and return immediately. Don't let him be left alone. He has a draught to take in case of necessity."

I turned back to the house with a sigh. I am afraid that I had as little faith in medicine as Guest himself.

CHAPTER XIV

GATHERING JACKALS

Guest for the remainder of the morning seemed to have fallen into a sort of stupor. He declined to sit in the garden or come down to lunch. When I went up to his room, he was lying upon a couch, half undressed, and with a dressing-gown wrapped around him. He opened his eyes when I came in, but waved me away.

"I am thinking," he said. "Don't interrupt me; I want to be alone for an hour or so."

"But you must have something to eat," I insisted. "You will lose your strength if you don't."

"Quite right," he admitted. "Send me up some soup, and let me have pencil and paper."

He was supplied with both. When I went up an hour later, he was smoking a cigarette and writing.

"I do not wish," he said, "to be worried with any more doctors. It is only a farce, and I have little time to spare."

"Nonsense!" I answered. "Rust declares that there is very little the matter with you. He has sent for a friend to come and have a look at you."

A little gesture of impatience escaped him.

"My dear Courage," he said, "I am obliged to you for all this care; but I am quite sure that, in your inner consciousness, you realize as I do that it is sheer waste of time."

He drew his dressing-gown a little closer around him. The hollows under his eyes seemed to have grown deeper since the morning.

"I am fairly run to earth," he continued. "Even these few hours of life I owe to my enemies. They hope to profit by them, of course. If you are the man I think you are, they will be mistaken. But don't waste my time with doctors."

He began to write again. I made some perfunctory remark which he entirely ignored. Just then I was called away. He watched my departure with obvious relief.

I was told that a stranger was waiting to see me in the library. My first thought was of the doctor. When I arrived there, I found a young man whose face was familiar, but whom I could not at once place. Then, like a flash, I remembered. It was the younger of the two men who had forced their way into my room at the Hotel Universal.

Now I was in no very good humor for dealing with these gentry. I had a distinct inclination to take him by the collar of the coat and throw him out. I fancy that he divined from my face how I was feeling, for he began hastily to explain his presence.

"I am very sorry to be an intruder, Mr. Courage," he said in his slow, precise English. "I had no wish to come at all. We were willing to leave you undisturbed. But we do not understand why you have sent for a doctor from London—and especially Professor Kauppmann!"

I looked at him deliberately. He was wearing English clothes—a dark tweed suit, ill-cut, and apparently ready-made; but the foreigner was written large all over him, from the tie of his bow to his narrow patent boots. His eyes were fixed anxiously upon me—large black eyes with long, feminine eyelashes. I think that if he had not been under the shelter of my own roof, I must have laid violent hands upon him.

"Why the devil should you understand?" I exclaimed. "Mr. Guest is my visitor, and if I choose to send for a doctor to see him, it is my business and nobody else's. If you have come here with any idea of bullying me, I am afraid you have wasted your time."

"You have evidently," he answered, "not troubled yourself to understand the situation! Mr. Guest is our prisoner!"

"Your what?" I exclaimed.

"Our prisoner," the young man answered. "Let me ask you this! Has Mr. Guest himself encouraged you in your attempt to interfere between him and his inevitable fate? No! I am sure that he has not! He accepts what he knows must happen! A few days more or less of life—what do they matter?"

"You make me feel inclined," I said grimly, "to test your theory."

The young man stepped back. My fingers were itching to take him by the throat, and I think that he read the desire in my face.

"Will you allow me to see Mr. Guest?" he asked.

"No! I'm d——d if I will," I answered. "I shall give you," I added, with my hand upon the bell, "exactly two minutes to leave this house."

The young man smiled superciliously, but he picked up his hat.

"I suppose, Mr. Courage, I must not blame you," he remarked, "You have all the characteristics of your country-people. You meet a delicate situation with the tactics of a bull!"

I laid my hand gently, but firmly upon his shoulder. We were half-way down the hall now, and the front door was wide open. I longed to throw him out, but I restrained myself. He was perfectly conscious, I am sure, of my inclination, but he showed no signs of uneasiness.

"I admit," I said calmly, "that you seem, all of you, to be engaged in proceedings of an extraordinary nature, which I do not in the least understand. But under my own roof, at any rate, I am master. I will not tolerate any interference with my guests; and as for Mr. Stanley from Liverpool and you, whatever you may call yourself, I will not have you near the place! You see my lodge gates," I added, pointing down the avenue, "I shall stand here until you have passed through them. If you come again, you will meet with a different reception!"

The young man laughed unpleasantly.

"Never fear, Mr. Courage," he answered. "Always we try first the simple means. If they should fail, we have many surer ways of gaining our ends. Au revoir!"

He left me and walked briskly off down the avenue. I fetched a pair of field-glasses, and watched him until he reached the lodge gates. A few moments later I saw him climb into a motor car, and vanish in a cloud of dust....

Later in the afternoon a victoria drew up before my front door just as I was starting for the village. Lady Dennisford leaned forward as I approached. She was closely veiled, but her voice shook with anxiety.

"How is he?" she asked.

"It is hard to say," I answered. "He has been writing for the last three hours. I was just going down to see if Rust has heard from the London man he wired for."

"Do you know why," she whispered, "he is so sure that he is going to die?"

I hesitated for a moment.

"He seems to imagine," I said, "that he has some enemies."

She sighed.

"I am afraid," she said, "that it is no imagination."

I looked at her in surprise.

"He has told me, perhaps," she said, a little hastily, "more than he has told you, and perhaps I am in a better position to understand. Mr. Courage, I wonder whether it would be possible for me to have an interview with any one of these men who are watching him."

"If you had been here a few hours ago," I said, "it would have been very possible indeed. One of them was here."

"What did he want?" she asked sharply.

"To see Mr. Guest, for one thing!"

"Did you allow it?"

"No! Guest is writing secrets with a loaded revolver by his side. He certainly does not want to see any of that crew."

"Oh! he is mad," she murmured. "Why should he not buy his life? What else is there that counts?"

"There are two to a bargain," I answered. "I do not think that he has value to give."

"Oh! he has," she answered, "if only he would be reasonable."

We were silent for a moment. In the distance, coming up the avenue, was the figure of a man. I watched him with curiosity. Finally I pointed him out to Lady Dennisford.

"Do you see this man coming up to the house?" I said—"a sleek, middle-aged man smoking a cigar?"

"I see him," she answered.

"What do you think he looks like?" I asked.

"A prosperous tradesman," she answered. "A friend of your bailiff's, perhaps."

"He calls himself Mr. Stanley from Liverpool," I answered, "and you can bargain with him for Guest's life."

"He is one of them!" she exclaimed.

"He is," I answered grimly, for I had good reason to know it.

She got out of the carriage at once.

"I am going to meet him," she said. "No! please let me go alone," she added, as I prepared to accompany her. "Afterwards we may need you."

I sent her carriage round to the stables, and I stood upon my steps watching her. Slim and elegant, she walked with swift level footsteps towards the approaching figure. I saw him shade his eyes with his hand as she approached; when she was within a few yards of him he took his cigar from his mouth and raised his hat. They stood for a moment or two talking; then Lady Dennisford turned, and they both came slowly towards the house. As they drew near me, she came on rapidly ahead.

"He is willing," she declared. "He will make terms. Where can we talk alone, we three?"

I led the way to my study. Mr. Stanley greeted me affably and with a commendable assumption of bluff respect.

"Fine place of yours, Mr. Courage," he declared. "Very fine place indeed. No wonder you prefer a country life. Finest thing in the world."

I made a pretence of answering him. But when we were in the study and the door was closed behind us, I felt that there was no longer any need to mince words.

"Mr. Stanley," I said, "Lady Dennisford says that you are willing to abandon your persecution of my guest for a consideration."

He smiled upon us slowly.

"Persecution," he remarked thoughtfully, "well, it is a harmless word. Mind, I admit nothing. But I am willing to hear what you have to say."

"This first, then," I declared. "Will you tell me why, as a magistrate of this county, I should not be justified in signing a warrant for your apprehension?"

"On what charge?" he asked.

"Conspiracy to murder," I answered.

He seemed to consider the suggestion with perfect seriousness.

"Yes!" he admitted, "it could be done. Putting myself in your place I should even imagine that it might be the most obvious course. But have you considered what the probable result would be?"

"It would keep you out of mischief for a time, at any rate."

"Not for a day," he answered softly. "In the first place, the slenderness of your evidence, which, by the by, when the affair came to trial would disappear altogether, would necessitate bail; and, in the second, were I to be swept off the face of the earth, there are thousands ready to take my place. Besides, no man likes to make himself the laughing stock of his friends and the press; and, forgive me, Mr. Courage, if I remind you that that is precisely what would happen in your case."

"Suppose, for a moment, then," said, "that I abandon that possibility. Make your own proposals. I do not know who you are or what you stand for. I do not know whether this is an affair of private vengeance, or whether you stand for others. That poor fellow upstairs cannot have a long life before him in any case. What is there we can offer you to leave him in peace?"

"You two—nothing," Mr. Stanley said gravely. "He himself can buy his life from us, if he wills."

"Then can I—or Lady Dennisford here," I asked, "be your ambassador? Can we tell him your terms?"

Mr. Stanley shook his head.

"It is impossible," he said. "Matters would have to be discussed between us which may not even be mentioned before any other person."

"You mean that you would have to see him alone?"

"Precisely!"

I turned to Lady Dennisford.

"He would never consent!" I declared.

"You must make him," she answered. "Mr. Courage!"

"Lady Dennisford!"

"Let me speak to you alone for a moment," she begged, laying her hand upon my arm. "Mr. Stanley will excuse us, I am sure."

80

"By all means," he declared, selecting an easy-chair.

"You will await us here?" I asked.

"Certainly!"

"On parole?"

"On parole, if you will give me a cigar."

I rang the bell for refreshments. Then Lady Dennisford and I left the room together.

CHAPTER XV

A DYING MAN

I had known Lady Dennisford for a good many years in a neighborly sort of way; but the woman who stood before me in the small sitting-room to which I had led her was a stranger to me. She had raised her veil; she was as pale as a woman may be, and her mouth, usually so firm and uncompromising, was now relaxed and tremulous. Before she spoke, I knew that tragedy was in the room with me. She tried to speak twice before the words came.

"Mr. Courage," she said, "may I speak to you as a friend?"

"Most certainly you can, Lady Dennisford," I answered.

I said and I meant it, for I was exceedingly sorry for her.

"Once I was to have married him," she said, "and I have cared for no one else all my life. There was a great scandal—a political scandal—and it was he upon whom the burden fell. His lips were sealed. I did not understand then, but I understand now. I sent him away! I joined with the others who persecuted him. And all the time—all the time he was innocent!"

Her last words were almost a wail. I was relieved to see that the tears were in her eyes at last.

"It was very hard fortune," I said awkwardly.

"His life has been one long exile," she said. "He has never married; he has been dead to the world for many years. His name, of course, is not Leslie Guest! If I dared tell you, you would understand I want him—oh! I want him so much to have a few years of happiness."

"What can we do, Lady Dennisford?" I asked earnestly.

"Take me up to him. Leave me with him alone."

I opened the door.

"At once!" I said.

He was still writing. The air of the room was thick with cigarette smoke. I opened the door gently, and Lady Dennisford glided past me. I myself hastened downstairs.

Mr. Stanley was apparently very comfortable. He was smoking one of my best cigars, and a whisky and soda stood at his elbow. He looked up from behind the *Times* as I entered.

"Lady Dennisford is with him," I said. "She will endeavor to persuade him to see you."

"Excellent!" he remarked. "Pray do not trouble to stay with me, if you have other matters to attend to. I have both time and patience to spare."

I went out into the garden. I began to feel the need of being alone. Events had marched rapidly with me during the last few hours and I was not used to such eruptions in my quiet life. I gave a few orders to my bailiff and gamekeeper, who were waiting to see me. I little guessed then how unimportant to me would be the prospects of the coming sport. It must have been nearly an hour before a servant found me, and announced that my guest desired to see me in his room. I hastened there at once.

Lady Dennisford was sitting at the table by Guest's side. She looked up as I entered, and I saw that the shadows lay deeper still upon her face.

"He chooses death!" she said simply.

He leaned over and touched her hand. His tone and manner had softened wonderfully.

"Eleanor," he said earnestly, "it is not I who choose. There is no choice! Your friend downstairs would say, 'Tell me all that you know of a certain matter, and the sentence which has been passed upon you shall be held over.' But when I had told him, when he knew everything, no agreement, no promise, could possibly be binding. I could not myself expect it. In his place I should make very sure that in a matter of hours I was a dead man. I say that myself, whose whole life has been sacrificed to a matter in which honor was largely concerned."

Lady Dennisford began to weep softly. He laid his hand upon hers.

"Are you sure, Mr. Guest," I said, "that you are not exaggerating the importance of this secret knowledge of yours? I dare say that Mr. Stanley, like every other man, has his price. If money—"

He interrupted me with a slight gesture of impatience.

"My young friend," he said, "I am not a poor man. Mr. Stanley is not to be dealt with as a single individual. He represents a system. I do not blame you for not being able to grasp these things. There is scarcely one Englishman in a thousand who would. I think that you have shown a great amount of trust as it is. Believe me now when I tell you that there are only two things in the world which can be done for me. The first is that you leave me a few minutes to say good-bye to Lady Dennisford; and the second that you keep every one away from me for one hour, while I Finish— these documents."

I left them alone! There was nothing else which I could do, and I waited in the hall below for Lady Dennisford.

When she came, she walked like a woman in a dream. Her veil was close drawn, and I could not see her face; but I was very sure that she had been weeping. I had already ordered her carriage round, and she took her place in it without a word.

I went back to the man whom I had left in the library.

He had lighted a fresh cigar, and was showing no signs of impatience.

"Our friend," I said, "has asked for one hour for consideration. If you will allow me, I should be pleased to show you the gardens and stables."

He accepted my offer at once, and proved himself an intelligent sightseer. He seemed to know a little about everything, including horses. I took him on to the orchid-houses, and it was quite an hour and a half before we returned to the house. I left him once more in the library, and I was on my way upstairs, when I came face to face with Rust and another man on their way down. For a moment I was speechless.

"Professor Kauppmann was unfortunately indisposed," Rust explained; "but he has sent this gentleman down—Dr. Kretznow, Mr. Courage. Curiously enough, Dr. Kretznow has already been called in to attend our friend upstairs."

"Mr. Courage no doubt remembers me," the newcomer remarked. "I am sorry to find our patient no better."

I looked him steadily in the face.

"You think that he will die?" I asked.

"I must admit," the doctor answered, "that I think he has very little chance of recovery. His constitution has gone. He has no recuperative powers."

Rust drew me a little on one side.

"You will be relieved to hear," he said, "that Dr. Kretznow considers his state quite a natural one. He does not encourage in any way the suspicions which, I must admit, I had formed."

84

"Indeed!" I answered.

"We are going to try an altogether new treatment," Rust continued, as we stood together upon the landing. "I think perhaps you ought to know, however, that our friend here gives very little hope."

I nodded.

"I shall leave you to entertain Dr. Kretznow," I said, "for a few minutes. I want to see Mr. Guest!"

I found him anxiously awaiting me. He had ceased writing but he held a roll of papers in his hand, and there was an ominous bulge in the pocket of his dressing-gown. He had more color than I had yet seen him with, and his eyes were unusually bright.

"For Heaven's sake come in, Courage, and close the door," he said irritably. "You see the result of your little doctor meddling with things he does not understand. I could have told you that no one would be allowed to enter these doors who might possibly give them away."

"We sent for Kauppmann," I explained.

"Of course! You will not realize what you are up against. You might as well have sent for the Angel Gabriel. Now will you do exactly as I ask you?"

"Go on," I said.

"Ring for your man and let him sit in the room with me. Go downstairs and get rid of those doctors. Then come up yourself, and be prepared to spend at least three hours here."

I obeyed him. I kept silent as to the fact that Stanley was in the house. I thought that he was already sufficiently excited. Downstairs I found that Dr. Kretznow was on the eve of departure. I did not seek to detain him for a moment. Rust, I think, wondered a little at my apparent lack of courtesy; but I almost bundled them out of the house.

He offered me his hand as he climbed up into the dog-cart, which I pretended, however, not to see.

"Mind, I give you very little hope, Mr. Courage," he said. "I studied the case very seriously in London, and I perceived symptoms which our friend here has not yet had the opportunity of observing. My own opinion is that his time is short."

"I am sorry to hear you say so, doctor," I answered; "for I quite believe that you are in a position to know."

He blinked at me for a moment from behind his thick spectacles, and I fancied that he was going to say something more. Apparently, however, he changed his mind, and the carriage drove off. I made my way at once into the library. Mr. Stanley was still awaiting me.

"My mission," I announced, "has been a failure. He declines even to discuss the matter."

Mr. Stanley knocked the ash off his cigar and rose to his feet. His face showed neither disappointment nor surprise.

"The lady, I am afraid," he remarked, "will be sorry."

"It will be a great blow to her," I answered, "if he should die!"

Mr. Stanley shrugged his shoulders.

"He will die, and very soon," he declared. "You and I know that very well. You are a young man, Mr. Courage," he added very slowly, and with his eyes fixed intently upon me. "You have a beautiful home and a simple, useful life—a long one, I trust—before you! Mr. Guest is not by any means old, but he made enemies! It is never wise to make enemies."

"Is this a warning?" I asked.

"Accept it as one, if a warning is necessary," he answered. "Take my advice. If Leslie Guest, or the man who is dying upstairs, has a legacy to leave, let him choose another legatee! There is death in that legacy for you!"

"Death comes to all of us," I answered. "We must take our risks."

He picked up his hat.

"Number 317, was it not?" he repeated thoughtfully, "an unlucky number for you, I fear! ... By the bye, Mademoiselle is in the neighborhood."

"What of it?" I asked.

He looked at me long and curiously. Then he sighed and lit still another of my finest Havanas as he prepared to depart.

"You will be better off," he said, "without that legacy!"

86

CHAPTER XVI

I TAKE UP MY LEGACY

Towards dawn I lit another lamp in my study and chanced to catch a glimpse of my face in a small mirror which stood upon my writing-table. Almost involuntarily I glanced over my shoulder, expecting to find another man there. It was a moment's madness, but as a matter of fact I did not recognize myself. It seemed to me that the change in the man upstairs, who had passed from the world of living things with breath in his body and life in his brain to the cold negation of death, was a change no greater than had come to me. For I was passing, as I knew very well, from behind the fences of my somewhat narrow but well-contained life into the great world of tragical happenings, where life and death are but small things, and one's self but a pawn in the great game. This, because I believed, because I had accepted the trust of the man who, a few hours ago, had closed his eyes with his hand in mine, and the faint welcoming smile upon his lips of a brave but weary man, who finds nothing terrible in death.

There was something almost fearful in a change so absolute and vital as that which had come over my life. I realized this as I allowed myself a few moments' rest, and threw myself upon the sofa. The old outlook, the old ideas had been torn up by the root. The things which had seemed to be of life itself only a few hours ago seemed now to have lapsed into the insignificance of trifles. I thought of myself and my old life with the tolerance of one who watches a child at play. Sport and all its kindred delights—the whole glorification of the physical life—I viewed as a Stock Exchange man might view the gambling for marbles of his youth. It was incredible that I had ever even fancied myself content. My brain was still in a whirl, but it seemed to me that I was already conscious of new powers. My thoughts travelled more quickly, I felt a greater alertness of brain, a swifter rush of ideas. But it seemed to me, also, that something had gone, that never again would I find my way lie through the rose gardens of life.

I must have dozed for a time upon the sofa, and was awakened by a soft tapping upon the low, old-fashioned windows, which opened upon the terrace. I sprang up, and, for a moment, it seemed to me that I must be dreaming. It was Adèle who stood there, all in white, with sunlight around her.... I gasped for a moment, and then recovered myself. It was Adèle sure enough, in a white linen riding habit, and morning had come while I slept. But I knew then that one link at least remained with the old life.

She tapped upon the window-pane a little imperiously, and I threw open the sash. Her eyes were fixed upon my face. I think that she, too, saw the change. With the opening of the window came a rush of sweet fresh air. She stepped into the room.

"Don't look at me as though I were something unreal!" she exclaimed. "I told them that I was fond of early morning rides, and I saw your light burning here from the park. Tell me—is he worse?"

I was suddenly calm. I realized that this was the beginning.

"He is dead," I answered. "He died about midnight."

There was a momentary horror in her face, for which I was grateful—I scarcely knew why.

"Dead," she repeated softly, "so soon!"

She looked around the room and back at me.

"Turn out the lamps," she said. "This light is ghastly."

There was little more color in her face than mine. Even the sunlight seemed cold and cheerless. She came a little nearer to me.

"He was conscious—at the end?"

"Yes!" I answered.

Her breath seemed to be coming a little faster. Her eyes were full of eager questioning.

"You were with him?"

"Yes!"

Again there was a pause. I was steadfastly silent.

"Don't keep me in suspense," she muttered. "He told you?"

"Yes!" I answered, "he told me—certain things."

She drew a long breath of relief. I could see that she was trembling all over. She sank into a chair.

"I felt that he would," she declared. "I knew that he could not carry his secret to the grave. Is the door locked?"

"Yes!" I answered. "The door is locked."

She was still pale, but her eyes were burning.

"Go on!" she said; "don't lose a moment. I am waiting."

"For what?" I asked calmly.

"To hear everything," she answered quickly.

"I have nothing to tell you," I said.

She stamped her foot with the petulance of a spoilt child.

"Oh! how dense you are!" she exclaimed. "Repeat to me exactly what he said to you—now, before you forget a single word!"

"I cannot do that," I said.

She leaned a little forward in her chair. Even then she did not understand.

"What do you mean?" she asked.

"I mean that the things which he told me with his last breath were for my own ear and my own knowledge alone," I answered. "I cannot share that knowledge even with you."

It seemed to me that there was something unreal, almost hideous, about the silence which followed. Through the open window there drifted into the room the early morning sounds of an awakening world—the whistling of birds in the shrubberies and upon the lawn, the more distant whir of a reaping machine at work in the cornfields. But between us—silence. I could not move my eyes from her face. There was no anger there, only a slowly dawning horror. She seemed to be looking upon me as a man doomed. I lit a match, and, taking some papers from my pocket, I slowly destroyed them.

"There go the last records," I said, blowing the ashes away, "I have learnt them by heart."

"I never thought of this," she murmured. "I never thought that you might be—oh! you cannot understand," she broke off. "You cannot know what you are doing."

"I have an idea," I answered grimly. "He warned me."

"Yet you cannot understand," she persisted. "Do you know that, even in saying this much to me, you are signing your death-warrant—that from this moment your life will not be safe for a single moment?"

"I know that there is danger," I answered; "but I am not an easy person to kill. I have had narrow escapes before, and escaped without a scratch."

She rose to her feet.

"If only I could make you understand," she muttered.

"Leslie Guest did his best," I answered. "He told me what the last few years of his life had been. I know that I have to face great odds. I can but do my best. We only die once."

Then she came swiftly over to me and laid her hands upon my shoulders. There was now something more human in her face. Her eyes seemed to plead with mine, and the joy of her near presence was a very real and subtle thing. I felt my eyes kindle and my heart beat fast. There was no other danger to be compared with this.

"I did not dream that this might happen," she said softly. "I meant to use you as a tool, I even thought that you had consented. Oh! I am sorry. I shall be sorry all my life that I asked you to bring him here. Will you listen to me for a moment?"

"I am listening all the time," I answered, taking one of her hands in mine.

"Have you realized what all this means?" she continued. "Are you prepared to give up your life here, your sports, your beautiful home, to feel that you have spies and enemies on every side, working always in the dark against you? The man who lies dead upstairs knew every move of the game—yet you see what has happened to him. How can you hope to succeed when he failed? Forget last night, my friend! I Believe that it was a nightmare, and I, too, will forget what you have told me. Come, it is not too late. We will say that he died suddenly in a stupor, and that, whatever his secrets were, he carried them with him. Is it agreed?"

I shook my head.

"One cannot break faith with the dead," I answered. "That is amongst the impossible things. Let us speak no more of it."

She leaned towards me. Her breath was upon my cheek, and her eyes shone into mine.

"Men have done more than this," she murmured, "when a woman has pleaded—- and—it is for your own sake. Think! Must I count you amongst my enemies?"

"God only knows why you should," I answered. "I am no judge of others; but if I betrayed the trust of a dead man, even for the sake of the woman I loved, I should put a bullet in my brain sooner or later. What I cannot understand, dear, is why you are not on my side. You are practically an Englishwoman. What have you to do with Leslie Guest's enemies?"

She turned away sadly.

"There are some things," she said, "which cannot be altered. You and I are on opposite sides. We may as well say good-bye. We shall never meet again like this."

"I cannot believe it," I answered. "There are many things which seem dark enough in the future to me, but I shall never believe that this is our good-bye."

It seemed to me strange afterwards, that of the immediate future neither of us spoke. I did not even ask her how long she was going to stay with Lady Dennisford; she did not speak to me of my plans. As she had come, so she went, silently and unexpectedly. She would not even let me follow her out onto the terrace; from the window I watched her mount her horse and ride away. Only just before she went she had looked back.

"I must see you again," she said. "You, too, must have time to think. I am going to forget this morning, I am going to forget that I have seen you. You, too, must do the same!"

Forget! She asked a hard thing.

CHAPTER XVII

NAGASKI'S INSTINCT

I was busy all the morning sending and receiving telegrams, and making certain plans on my own account. Rust was with me a good deal of the time; but the visitor whose coming I was expecting every minute did not arrive till early in the afternoon. I sent out word to Mr. Stanley that I was exceedingly busy, and should be glad to be excused; but, as I had confidently expected, he was insistent. In about a quarter of an hour I received him in the library.

He sank softly into the chair towards which I had pointed. For a moment he sat and blinked at me behind his gold-rimmed spectacles.

"So our friend," he murmured, "has passed away! It is very sad—very sad indeed."

I leaned back in my chair and regarded him steadfastly.

"Mr. Stanley," I said, "you did not come here to express your sympathy with the man whom you have done your best, if not to kill, at least to frighten to death. Ask me all the questions you want to—say anything you think necessary. Only finish it up. When you leave this room, let me feel that circumstances will not require any further meeting between us."

My words seemed to afford Mr. Stanley matter for thought. His brows were slightly puckered. I knew that from behind his glasses I was being subjected to a very keen examination.

"I only trust, Mr. Courage,"' he said softly, "that the wish you have expressed may become a possibility. I myself have always regretted your intervention in this affair. You are, if you will forgive my saying so, in strange waters."

"I don't know about that," I answered curtly. "I don't see now how I could have done other than I have done. But anyhow, I'm sick of it. I don't want to seem discourteous, but if you could manage to say to me, in the course of a quarter of an hour, all that you have to say, and ask all the questions you want to, I should be glad to have done with the whole business, once and for all!"

My visitor nodded thoughtfully.

"Very good, Mr. Courage," he said. "I will endeavor to imitate your frankness. Is there to be a post-mortem?"

"There is not," I answered. "Dr. Rust does not consider it necessary, and I am forced to confess that I cannot see anything to be gained by it. You and your friends may have been responsible for his death. I cannot say! At any rate, I am sure that we should never be able to fix the guilt in the proper quarter."

Mr. Stanley shrugged his shoulders slightly.

"I must congratulate you upon your common sense, Mr. Courage," he said. "I pass on now to a more important question. Did our friend, before he died, impart to you any of the hallucinations under which he suffered? Are you his legatee?"

"I am not," I answered. "I believe that he meant me to be; but his death, when it came, was quite sudden. All the secret information I had from him was his name, and the address of his lawyers."

There was a short silence. I was able to bear with perfect calmness the keen scrutiny to which my visitor was subjecting me.

"I congratulate you heartily, Mr. Courage," he said at last. "Mr. Guest's story, if he had told it to you, would have been a mixture of stolen facts and hallucinations, which might have influenced your life very forcibly for evil. I wished for his death! I admit it freely. But I wished it for this reason: because in all Europe yesterday, there did not breathe a more dangerous man than the man who called himself Leslie Guest."

"Well, he has gone," I said, "and his life, so far as I know of it, has been a very sad one. I have already explained to you my wishes in the matter. I want to forget as speedily as possible the events of the last eight days."

"I should like," Mr. Stanley said, "to see him."

"I am sorry," I answered, "but that is impossible. The nurses are busy in the room now, and apart from that, the dead, at least, should have peace from their enemies. Of one thing I can assure you. Every scrap of paper he had with him is burnt. There is nothing about him or the room which could be of interest to you. I have sent for his lawyer, and am making arrangements for the funeral. There is nothing more to be said or done, except to say good afternoon to you, Mr. Stanley,"

He rose slowly up from his chair.

"You are a little precipitate, Mr. Courage," he said, "but I do not know that I can blame you. Do you object to telling me when the funeral will be?"

"I am not myself informed, at present," I answered. "I am waiting for the arrival of the lawyer."

I had risen to my feet, and was standing with the handle of the door in my hand. Mr. Stanley took the hint, yet I fancied that he departed unwillingly.

"I should like," he admitted, "to have seen—him, and also the lawyer."

"Then you can find another opportunity," I answered stiffly. "Mr. Guest's friends would receive every consideration from me. His enemies, I must admit, I cannot, under the circumstances, see the back of too quickly."

Mr. Stanley had no alternative but to depart, which he did with as good a grace as possible. I was glad to be alone for a few minutes. My ordinary share of the vices of life, both great and small, I was, without a doubt, possessed of. But I had never been a liar. I had never looked a man in the face and made statements which I had known at the time were absolutely and entirely false. This was my first essay in a new rôle.

My next visitor was a very different sort of person, a fair, florid little man, with easy, courteous manners, and dressed in deep mourning. He introduced himself as Mr. Raynes, of Raynes and Bishop, Solicitors, Lincoln's Inn, and alluded to the telegram which I had sent him earlier in the morning.

"May I inquire," he asked, after we had exchanged a few commonplaces, "if you are aware that Mr. Leslie Guest was an assumed name of the deceased?"

"I was in his confidence towards the last," I answered. "He told me a good deal of his history."

The lawyer nodded sympathetically.

"A very sad one, I fear you found it," he remarked.

"Very sad indeed," I assented.

"I have here," he continued, "Lord Leslie's will, and instructions as to his burial. I presume you would like me to take entire charge of all the arrangements?"

"Certainly," I answered.

"His Lordship wished to be buried very quietly in the nearest churchyard to the place where he died," the lawyer continued. "I presume that can be arranged."

"Quite easily," I answered. "The clergyman is waiting to see you now; if you like I will take you to him."

In the hall we met Lady Dennisford. She was plainly dressed in black, and she carried a great bunch of white roses. I introduced Mr. Raynes to the vicar, and hurried back to her.

"You would like to see him?" I asked.

She nodded, and I led the way upstairs. I opened the door and closed it again softly, leaving them alone....

I descended into the hall, and there upon the steps, looking at me with black, beady eyes, deep set in his wrinkled face, was my friend, or rather my enemy, Nagaski. He eyed my approach with gloomy disfavor. He opened his mouth in a seeming yawn, a little, red tongue shot out from between his ivory teeth. Then I heard him called by a familiar voice, and passing out, I found his mistress leaning back in the corner of Lady Dennisford's victoria.

She welcomed me with a slow, curious smile.

"I will get out," she said. "There is something I should like to say to you."

I handed her down. She led the way on to the terrace. A few paces behind, Nagaski, with drooping head and depressed mien, followed us. When we halted, he sat upon his haunches and watched me.

"Nagaski," I remarked, "does not seem to be quite himself to-day."

"It is your presence," she answered, "which affects him. He dislikes you."

I looked at him thoughtfully. If Nagaski disliked me, I was very sure that I returned the sentiment to a most unreasonable extent.

"I wonder why," I said. "I have always been decent to him."

"Nagaski has antipathies," she said quietly. "It is a good thing that we are not in his own country. There his breed are supposed to have some of the qualities of seers, and his dislike would be a very ominous thing."

"Are you superstitious?" I asked.

"I am not sure," she answered gravely. "If I were, I should certainly avoid you. His attitude is a distinct warning."

I drew a little nearer to her. It seemed to me that she was very pale, and there was trouble in her face.

"Do you think it possible?" I asked, "that I could bring sorrow upon you?"

"Very possible indeed," she murmured, avoiding my eyes, and looking steadily across the park.

"Since when have you discovered this?" I asked.

"Within the last hour," she answered.

I laid my hand upon hers. She withdrew it at once. There was a distinct change in her manner towards me.

"I suppose," she remarked, "that I ought to congratulate you. You are certainly cleverer than I gave you credit for. You have deceived Mr. Stanley, and he is not at all an easy person for a beginner to deceive."

I kept silence. I began to see the trouble into which I was drifting.

"But," she continued, "you did not attempt to deceive me. And in this matter, Mr. Stanley and I are one!"

"You have told him!" I exclaimed.

"Not yet," she answered, "but I am forced to do so, unless—"

"Unless what?"

She looked me in the face.

"Unless you give me your word of honor that you make no attempt to carry on the task which Leslie Guest had assigned himself, that you do not regard yourself in any shape or form as his successor. Don't you see that it must be so? You plead that you must keep faith with the dead. I, at least, must keep faith with the living. I offer you a chance of safety, and I beg you to take it. I can do no more."

There was a sharp, little yap from Nagaski. We looked around, Lady Dennisford had come out. We turned towards her. Nagaski trotted on ahead. His demeanor was generally more brisk, and his expression one of relief. A cloud of anxiety seemed to have rolled away from his small brain. Adèle pointed to him significantly.

"You see," she said, "his instinct is right. There are evil things between you and me. If I speak, there is no hope for you, and if I keep silent, there is danger for me, and I am a woman forsworn. If only I had never gone to Lord's and seen you play cricket!"

96

"Would that have helped us?" I asked.

"Of course! I should never have counted upon you as a possible tool! I saw you strain every nerve in your body to catch a ball, and I judged you by your pursuits, and—all this has come of it. Nagaski was right. We go ill together, you and I, and one of us must suffer."

"I can only pray then," I answered, as I handed her into the carriage, "that it may be I."

Nagaski sprang upon his mistress' lap, and his was the only farewell I received as the carriage drove away. His upper lip was drawn back over his red gums; there was something fiendish and uncanny in his snarl, and the hatred which shone from his tiny black eyes. I watched the carriage until it disappeared. He had not moved. He was still looking back at me.

CHAPTER XVIII

IN THE DEATH CHAMBER

I sat up suddenly in bed and turned on the light. It was barely two o'clock by my watch, but I felt sure that I had not been mistaken. Some one had knocked at my door.

In the act of springing out of bed the sound was repeated. This time there was certainly no mistake about it, and I heard my name called—

"Mr. Courage! Mr. Courage!"

I opened the door. The landing was dimly lit, and I could see little else except the figure of the woman who stood there. With one hand she was leaning against the wall, her face was as white as a sheet; she wore a hastily thrown on dressing-gown of dingy red. Her whole appearance was that of a person convulsed with fright.

"Who are you?" I asked. "What do you want?"

Her lips parted. She seemed to have the intention of speaking, but no words came. Her teeth began to chatter.

"Come," I said brusquely, "you must—why you are the nurse whom Dr. Rust sent, aren't you?" I asked, suddenly recognizing her. "What is the matter with you? Are you ill?"

All the time, although she was silent, her eyes, distended and terror-stricken, were fixed upon me. She nodded feebly.

"Something—is wrong!" she faltered at last. "Come!"

She turned away, still with one hand holding on to the wall. She evidently wished me to follow her.

"One moment," I said. "Wait while I put something on."

I turned back into my room and wrapped my dressing-gown around me. Then I followed her along the corridor. She led the way to the room which had been occupied by Leslie Guest. Outside the door she hesitated. She turned and faced me abruptly. She was white to the lips. Her appearance was horrible.

"I dare not go in!" she moaned. "I have been a nurse for fifteen years, and I have never known anything like this!"

"Like what?" I asked, bewildered. "What is it that has happened?"

She shivered, but she did not answer me. I was beginning to feel impatient.

"Are you hysterical?" I asked. "I wish you would try and tell me what is the matter."

"Go in," she answered; "go in, and see—if you can see anything."

I opened the door and entered. The room was dimly lit by a lamp, placed on the table near the window. Upon the bed, covered by a sheet, his waxen-like face alone visible, was the body of the man who had been my guest. Beyond, with the connecting door wide open, was the anteroom where the nurse had been sleeping. Except for the ticking of a clock, there was no sound to be heard; there was no sign anywhere of any disturbance or disorder. I looked back at the nurse for an explanation.

"What is it that has upset you so?" I asked. "I can see nothing wrong."

She pointed to the bed.

"His eyes!" she murmured. "Go and look!"

I walked over to the bedside, and leaned reverently over the still figure. Suddenly I felt as though I were turned to stone. The blood in my veins ran cold, I staggered back. My gaze had been met with an upturned glassy stare from a pair of wide-opened, deep-set eyes!

"Good God!" I cried, "his eyes are open!"

The nurse, who had gained a little courage, came to my side.

"I closed them myself," she whispered. "I closed them carefully. I thought that I heard a noise and I came in. I lit a lamp and I saw—what you can see! Fifteen years I have been a nurse, and I have watched by the dead more times than I can count. But I have never known that happen!"

Once more I approached the bedside. One arm was drawn up a little from under the clothes. I noticed its somewhat unnatural position and pointed it out to the nurse.

"Did you leave it like that?" I asked.

Her teeth chattered.

"No!" she answered, "The arms were quite straight. Some one has been in the room—or—"

99

"Or what?" I asked.

"He must have moved," she whispered in an unnatural tone.

Once more I bent over the still form. The pupils of the wide-open eyes were slightly dilated; they seemed to meet mine with a horrible, unseeing directness. There was no sign about his waxen face or still, cold mouth that life had lingered for a moment beyond the stated period. And yet something of the nurse's terror was slowly becoming communicated to me. I felt that I was in close company with mysterious things.

I turned towards the nurse.

"Go to your room," I said, "and shut yourself in there. I am going to send for Dr. Rust. Understand it is you that are ill. I do not want a word of this to be spoken of amongst the servants."

She passed into her room and closed the door without a word. I had a telephone from my room to the stables, and in a few moments I had succeeded in awakening one of the grooms.

"The nurse is ill," I told him. "Take a dog-cart and go down and fetch Dr. Rust. Ask him to come back with you at once."

I heard his answer, and a few minutes later the sound of wheels in the avenue. Then I put on my clothes, and going downstairs, fetched some brandy and took it up to the nurse. She, too, was dressed; and, although she was still pale, she had recovered her self-possession.

"I am very sorry to have been so foolish, sir," she said, declining the brandy. "I have never had an experience like this before, and it rather upset me."

"You think," I asked, "that he has lived, since—"

"I am sure of it," she answered. "His was a very peculiar illness, and I know that it puzzled the doctor very much. It was just the sort of illness to have led to a case of suspended animation."

"You think it possible," I asked, "that he is alive now?"

"It is quite possible," she answered, "but not very likely. He probably died with the slight effort he made in moving his arm. I am quite willing to go in and examine him, if you like, or would you prefer to wait until the doctor comes?"

"We will wait," I answered. "He cannot be more than a few minutes."

Almost as I spoke, I heard the dog-cart returning. I hurried downstairs and admitted the doctor. It was almost daybreak and very cold. A thin, grey mist hung over the park; a few stars were still visible. Eastwards, there was a faint break in the clouds.

"What's wrong?" he asked, as I closed the door behind him.

"Something very extraordinary, doctor," I answered, hurrying him upstairs. "Come and hear what the nurse has to say."

He looked at me in a puzzled manner, but I hurried him upstairs. The nurse met him on the landing. She whispered something in his ear, and they entered the bedchamber together. I remained outside.

In about ten minutes the door was thrown open, and the doctor appeared upon the threshold. He was in his shirt-sleeves, and there was a look upon his face which I had never seen there before. He had the appearance of a man who has been in touch with strange things.

"Some hot water," said he—"boiling, if possible. Don't ask me any questions, there's a good fellow!"

I had already aroused some of the servants, telling them that the nurse had been taken ill, and I was able to bring what he had asked for in a few minutes. But when I returned with it and tried the handle of the door, I found it locked. Rust opened it after I had knocked twice, and took the can from me.

"Go away, there's a good fellow," he begged. "I will come to you as soon as I can—as soon as there is anything to tell."

I obeyed him without demur. I went into my study, ordered some tea, and tried to read. It must have been an hour before the door was opened, and Rust appeared.

"Courage," he said, "I have some extraordinary news for you."

"I am quite prepared for it," I answered calmly.

"He is alive!"

I nodded.

"I judged as much."

"More than that! I believe he will recover!"

There was a short silence. I had never seen Rust so agitated.

101

"You don't seem to grasp quite all that this means," he continued. "For the first time in my life, I have signed a certificate of death for a living person!"

"You have signed the certificate?" I asked.

He nodded.

"The undertaker has it."

The maid entered just then with the tea. I ordered another cup for Rust, and when it had arrived, I made him sit down opposite to me.

"His was exactly the kind of illness," he remarked thoughtfully, "to lead to something of this sort. I am quite sure now, whatever Kauppmann's friend may say, that his disease was not a natural one. He has been suffering from some strange form of poisoning. It is the most interesting case I have ever come in contact with. There were certain symptoms—"

"Rust," I interrupted, "forgive me, but I don't want to hear about symptoms. I want to talk to you as man to man. We are old friends! You must listen carefully to what I have to say."

Rust's good-humored, weather-beaten, little face was almost pitiful.

"You're going to pitch into me, of course," he remarked. "Well, I suppose I deserve it. You may not believe it, but I can assure you that ninety-nine out of every hundred medical men would have signed the certificate in my case."

"I have no doubt of it," I answered. "That is not the matter I want to discuss with you at all. There is something more serious, terribly serious, behind all this. Frankly, if I did not know you so well, Rust, I should offer you the biggest fee you had ever received in your life, to leave the place this morning and be called to—- Timbuctoo. As it is," I continued more slowly, "I am going to appeal to you as a sportsman! I am going to take you into my confidence as far as I dare. I want, if I can, to justify a very extraordinary request."

Rust took off his spectacles and laid them upon the table.

"The request being—" he asked.

"That you start for the holiday you were speaking of the other day," I said, "within twelve hours."

He glanced at me curiously. I think that he was beginning to wonder whether I might not be the next person to need medical advice.

102

"Go on," he said. "I am prepared to listen at any rate...."

He listened. And at 10.30 that morning, he left Saxby—for the South Coast.

CHAPTER XIX

AN AFFAIR OF STATE

My cousin met me at St. Pancras. I saw him before my own carriage had reached the platform, peering into the window of every compartment in his short-sighted way. He recognized me at last with a little wave of the hand.

"Glad to see you, Hardross! These your things? We'll have a hansom. Where are you staying?"

"At the club, if I can get a room," I answered. "I shall try there before I go to an hotel, at any rate."

"Come and have some lunch first," Sir Gilbert said firmly. "You can see about your room afterwards. Remember your appointment is at three o'clock."

I acquiesced, and got into a cab with my cousin. I was perfectly aware that he was almost consumed with curiosity. He scarcely waited until we were off before he began.

"Hardross!" he asked, "what's up?"

"Nothing particular," I answered lamely.

"Rubbish!" he declared, "you are the last man in the world I should have expected to see in town the second week in September! You haven't come for nothing, have you? And then this interview with Lord Polloch. What on earth can you have to say to the Prime Minister?"

"I'm afraid, Gilbert," I answered, "that I can't tell you—just yet. You see it isn't my own affair at all. It's—another man's secret."

My cousin was palpably disappointed.

"Well," he said, a little curtly, "whatever sort of a secret it is, it hasn't agreed with you very well. I never saw you look so seedy—and years older too! What on earth have you been doing with yourself?"

I shrugged my shoulders.

"I've had a cold," I said. "Got wet through shooting one day last week."

My cousin regarded me incredulously.

"A cold! You!" he remarked. "I like that! I don't believe you ever had such a thing in your life!"

I leaned forward in the cab to look at the placards of the afternoon papers.

"Any news in town?" I asked.

"None at all," Gilbert answered. "There's scarcely any one about. I'm off to Hamburg to-morrow myself."

"And Lord Polloch?" I asked.

"He's off to Scotland to-night for a fortnight's golf. Afterwards I believe he's going abroad. You must confess that your appearance here is a little extraordinary. If I hadn't been on particularly good terms with Polloch, I could not possibly have got you an interview. He's up to his eyes in work, and as keen as a schoolboy on getting away for his holiday."

"It's very good of you," I answered.

My cousin regarded me critically.

"You'll forgive my suggesting it, I'm sure, Hardross," he said, "but you have got something particular to say to him, I suppose? These fellows don't like being bothered about trifles. The responsibility is on my shoulders, you see."

"I have something quite important to say to him," I declared. "In all probability, he will give you a seat in the Cabinet for having arranged the meeting."

Gilbert abandoned the subject for the moment. A sense of humor was not amongst his characteristics, and I do not think that he approved altogether of my levity. But later on, as we sat at luncheon, he returned to it.

"Have you ever thought of Parliament, Hardross?" he asked.

I shook my head.

"One in the family," I murmured, "is sufficient."

"The diplomatic service," he remarked, "you are, of course, too old for."

"Naturally," I agreed; "as a matter of fact, I have no hankerings for what you would call a career."

"And yet—" he began.

"And yet," I interrupted, "I am anxious for an interview with the Prime Minister. I am afraid I cannot tell you very much, Gilbert, but I will tell you this. Some rather important information has come into my possession in a very curious fashion. I conceive it to be my duty to pass it on to the government of this country. Lord Polloch can decide whether or not it is of any real value. It is for this purpose that I am seeking this interview with him. I tell you this much in confidence. I cannot tell you more."

My cousin smiled in a somewhat superior manner.

"You have got a cheek," he said. "As though any information you could pick up would be worth bothering Polloch with!"

I glanced at the clock and leaned back in my chair.

"Well," I said, "in about a quarter of an hour his Lordship will have an opportunity of judging for himself. By the bye, Gilbert, do you mind keeping what I have told you entirely to yourself?"

"You haven't told me anything," he grunted.

"I have told you enough to get me into pretty considerable trouble," I remarked grimly. "Shall I see you later?"

"I shall wait till you return," he answered firmly. "I am rather anxious to hear how you get on with the chief."

"I am a little anxious about it myself," I admitted, as we went out into the hall.

I walked the short distance to Downing Street. The afternoon was brilliantly fine, and the pavements were thronged with foot-passengers. I passed down the club steps into what seemed to me to be a new world. I did not recognize myself or my kinship with my fellow-creatures. For the first time in my life, I was affected with forebodings. I scanned the faces of the passers-by. I had an uneasy suspicion all the time that I was watched. As I turned in to Downing Street, the feeling grew stronger. There were several loiterers in the roadway. I watched them suspiciously. The idea grew stronger within me that I should not be allowed to reach my destination. I found myself measuring the distance, almost counting the yards which separated me from that quiet, grey stone house, almost the last in the street. It was with a sense of immense relief that I pushed open the gate and found myself behind the high iron palings. A butler in sombre black opened the door, almost before my hand had left the bell. I was myself again immediately. My vague fears melted away. I handed in my card, and explained that I had an appointment with Lord Polloch. In less than five minutes I was ushered into his presence.

"I am very glad to see you, Mr. Courage," he said. "I understand that you have some information which you wish to give me. I have exactly twenty-five minutes to give you. Take that easy-chair and go ahead...."

In less than three-quarters of an hour, I was back in the club. I found my cousin almost alone in the smoking-room. He looked up with ill-suppressed eagerness as I entered.

"Well?"

I lit a cigarette and threw myself into an easy-chair.

"Quiet afternoon here?" I remarked.

"You saw Lord Polloch?"

I nodded.

"I was with him exactly twenty-five minutes," I answered.

"Well?" he repeated.

I called a waiter and ordered something to drink. I felt that I needed it.

"My dear Gilbert," I said, "I will not affect to misunderstand you! You want to know how Lord Polloch received me, what the nature of my business with him was, and its final result. That is so, isn't it?"

"To a certain extent, yes!" he admitted; "as I was responsible for the interview, I naturally feel some interest in it," he added stiffly.

"Lord Polloch was most civil," I assured him. "He thanked me very much for coming to see him. He hoped that I would call again immediately on his return from Scotland, and—I have no doubt that by this time he has forgotten all about me."

"Your information, after all, then," Gilbert exclaimed, "was not really important!"

"He did not appear to find it so," I admitted.

"I wonder," Gilbert said, looking at me curiously "what sort of a mare's nest you have got hold of. Rather out of your line, this sort of thing, isn't it?"

The walls of the club smoking-room seemed suddenly to break away. I was looking out into the great work where men and women faced the whirlwinds, and were torn away, struggling and fighting always, into the Juggernaut of destruction. I looked into the quiet corners where the cowards lurked, and I seemed to see my own empty place there.

"Oh! I don't know," I answered calmly. "We are all the slaves of opportunity. Lord Polloch very courteously, but with little apparent effort, has made me feel like a fool. Perhaps I am one! Perhaps Lord Polloch is too much of an Englishman. That remains to be discovered."

"What do you mean by 'too much of an Englishman'?" Gilbert asked.

I shrugged my shoulders.

"Too much self-confidence, too little belief in the possibility of the unusual," I answered.

"Suppose you appoint me arbitrator," Gilbert suggested.

I shook my head.

"I cannot, Gilbert," I answered. "As I have said, the issue is between Lord Polloch and myself, and I hope to Heaven that Lord Polloch is in the right, or there will be trouble."

"You are extraordinarily mysterious," Gilbert remarked.

"I must seem so," I answered, "I cannot help it. Have a drink, Gilbert, and wish me God speed!"

"Are you off back to Medchestershire to-night?" Gilbert asked.

I shook my head.

"No! but I thought of running over to the States next week."

Gilbert laid down his cigar, and looked at me anxiously.

"Have you seen a doctor lately, Hardross?" he asked.

"Not necessary," I answered. "I'm as fit as I can be!"

"Then will you tell me," he asked, "why, with the shooting just on, and the hunting in full view, you are talking of going to America?"

108

"I've had a good many years of hunting and shooting and cricket and sport of all sorts, Gilbert," I answered. "Perhaps I'm not quite so keen as I was."

"If you are not going to America for sport," my cousin asked, "what are you going for?"

I rose to my feet.

"Gilbert," I said, "it's no use. Some day or other you will know all about it—-perhaps very soon. But, for the present, I can tell you nothing. I've stumbled into a queer place, and I've got to get out of it somehow. Wish me good luck, old chap!" I added, holding out my hand; "and—if anything should happen to me abroad—look after the old place—it'll be yours, you know, every stick and stone."

Then I got away as soon as I could. Gilbert was by way of becoming incoherent, and, so far as I was concerned, there was nothing more to be said.

CHAPTER XX

TRAVELLING COMPANIONS

I locked the door of my state-room, and seated myself upon the edge of the lower bunk with a little sigh of relief. The slow pounding of the engines had commenced, the pulse of the great liner was beating, and through the port-hole I could see the docks, with their line of people, gliding past us. We were well out in the Mersey already.

"We're off, Guest!" I exclaimed, "and off safely, too, I think. Chuck that now, there's a good fellow."

Guest was engaged in emptying the contents of one of my bags. He turned slowly round and faced me, with a pair of my trousers upon his arm.

"I shall do nothing of the sort," he answered calmly. "I am here as your servant, Courage, and your servant I intend to remain. We can't hope to keep the thing up on the other side, if we are all the time drifting back to our old relations. I wish I could make you understand this."

I opened the port-hole as far as it would go, and lit a cigarette.

"That's all very well," I said; "but I don't see any need to keep the farce up in private, and I'm sure I can unpack my own things a thundering sight better than you can."

"Very likely," he answered, "but you certainly won't do it. Can't you understand that, unless we grow into our parts, they will never come naturally to us? Besides, we may be watched. You cannot tell."

"The door is locked," I remarked dryly.

"For the moment, no doubt, we're all right," Guest answered; "but you won't be able to lock it often upon the voyage. Remember that we are up against a system with a thousand eyes and a thousand ears. It's no good running risks. I am Peters, your man, and Peters I mean to be."

"Do you propose," I asked, "to have your meals in the servants' saloon?"

"Most certainly I do," was the curt answer. "I expect to make acquaintances there who will be most useful. Did you get the passengers' list?"

I drew it from my pocket. Guest came and looked over my shoulder. Half-way down the list he pointed to a name.

"Mr. de Valentin and valet!" he murmured. "That is our friend. I recognize the name. He has used it before! Now let us see."

Again his forefinger travelled down the list—again it paused.

"Mrs. Van Reinberg, and the Misses Van Reinberg! Ah!" he said, "that is the lady whose acquaintance you must contrive to make."

"One of the court?" I asked,

He nodded.

"There are others, of course, but I do not recognize their names. They will sort themselves up naturally enough. Now unlock that door, and go up on deck. The stewards will be in directly for orders."

I rose and stretched out my hand towards the door. Suddenly, from outside, an unexpected sound almost paralyzed me—the sharp, shrill yapping of a small dog!

I felt the color leave my cheeks. Guest looked at me in amazement.

"What's the matter with you?" he asked. "You're not frightened of a toy terrier, are you?"

I opened the door. Of course, my sudden fear had been absurd. I peered out into the passage, and a little exclamation broke from my lips. Sitting on his haunches just outside, his mouth open, his little, red tongue hanging out, was a small Japanese spaniel. There may have been thousands of others in the world, but that one I was very sure, from the first, that I recognized, and I was equally sure that he recognized me. I stared at him fascinated. His bead-like, black eyes blinked and blinked again; and his teeth, like a row of ivory needles, gleamed white from his red gums. He neither growled nor wagged his tail, but it seemed to me that the expression of his aged, puckered-up little face was the incarnation of malevolence. I pointed to him, and whispered hoarsely to Guest:

"Her dog!"

"Whose?" he asked sharply.

"Miss Van Hoyt's," I answered.

"Rubbish!" he declared. "There are hundreds of dogs like that."

I shook my head.

"Never another in the wide world," I said. "Look how the little brute is scowling at me!"

The bedroom steward came round the corner at that moment. I pointed to the dog.

"I always understood that dogs were not permitted in the state-rooms, steward," I remarked.

"They are not, sir," the man answered promptly. "The young lady to whom this one belongs has a special permission; but he is not allowed to be out alone. He must have run away."

There was the sound of rustling petticoats. A young woman in black came hurrying down the passage. She caught up the dog without a word, and hastened away.

"At what time would you like to be called, sir?" the man asked.

"Send me the bath-room steward, and I will let you know," I answered, stepping back into the state-room.

"He'll be round in a few minutes, sir," the man answered, and passed on.

Guest leaned towards me. His eyes were bright and alert, and his manner was perfectly composed. He was more used to such crises than I was. He asked no question; he waited for me to speak.

"It was her maid!" I exclaimed. "I was sure of the dog."

"Miss Van Hoyt's?"

"Yes!"

He caught up the passengers list. There was no such name there.

"If it is she," he said quietly, "she is here to watch you! It proves nothing else. I shall be seasick all the way over, and at New York we must part. Go to the purser's office and find out, Courage. There is no reason why you shouldn't. You are interested, of course?"

I nodded and left the state-room, but I had no need to visit the purser. I met her face to face coming out of the saloon. If appearances were in any way to be trusted, the meeting was as much a shock to her as to me. She was wearing a thick veil, which partially obscured her features, but I saw her stop short, and clutch at a pillar as though for support, as she recognized me. If the amazement in her tone was counterfeited, she was indeed an actress.

"You!" she exclaimed. "Where are you going?"

"America, I hope," I answered. "And you? I did not see your name on the passengers' list."

"I am going—home," she answered. "I made up my mind, at the last moment, to come on this steamer, to cross with my stepmother."

I did not like the way she said it. It was too apt—a little too mechanical. And yet I could not get it out of my head that her surprise was natural.

A little, fair woman, wearing a magnificent fur cloak, and with an eyeglass dangling at her bosom, suddenly bore down upon us.

"Adèle!" she exclaimed, "have you seen my woman? I've forgotten the number of my state-room."

"It is opposite mine," Adèle answered. "I can show it to you."

They passed on together. The fair, little lady had favored me with a very perfunctory and somewhat insolent glance; Adèle herself left me without a word. I went into the saloon, took my place for dinner, and then sought the deck for some fresh air. I felt that I needed it.

A slight, drizzling rain was falling, but I took no notice of it. I walked backwards and forwards along the promenade deck, my pipe in my mouth, my hands clasped behind me. The appearance of Adèle had been so utterly unexpected that I felt myself almost unnerved. For six days we should be living in the close intimacy which fellow passengers upon a steamer find it almost difficult to avoid. Our opportunities for conversation would be practically unlimited. If indeed Guest's suspicions as to the reason of her presence here were well founded, a single slip on my part might mean disaster. And yet, beneath it all, I knew quite well that her near presence was a delight to me! My blood was running more warmly, my heart was the lighter for the thought of her near presence. Danger might come of it, the success of our undertaking itself might be imperilled—yet I was glad. I leaned over the vessel's side, and gazed through the gathering twilight at the fast receding shores, with their maze of yellow lights. Life had changed for me during the last few weeks. The old, placid days of content were over; already I was in a new world, a world of bigger things, where the great game was being played, with the tense desperateness of those who gamble with life and death. I had not sought the change! Rather it had been forced upon me. I had no ambitions to gratify; the old life had pleased me very well. I had quitted it simply upon compulsion. And here I was with unfamiliar thoughts in my brain, groping my way along paths which were strange to me, face to face now with the greatest happening which Heaven or Hell can let loose upon a man. It was a queer trick this, which fortune had played me.

After all we are very human. The dressing bugle brought me back to the present, and I remembered that I was hungry. I descended into my state-room, and found all my things neatly laid out, and Guest sitting on the opposite bunk regarded them critically.

"You shouldn't have bothered about my clothes, Guest," I protested.

"Nonsense," he answered curtly. "I can't play the part without a few rehearsals. What about Miss Van Hoyt?"

"She is on board," I answered.

"You have spoken to her?"

"Yes!"

"Did she offer any explanations as to her presence?"

"She appeared to be surprised to see me," I answered. "She said that she was going home."

Guest nodded thoughtfully.

"Her stepmother is an American," he remarked. "I don't suppose you knew that?"

"I did not," I admitted. "I wish you would tell me all that you know of Miss Van Hoyt."

"No time now," he answered. "You will be late for dinner as it is. Don't seem too eager about it, but remember it is absolutely necessary that you get an introduction to Mrs. Van Reinberg."

I nodded.

"I'll do my best," I promised.

CHAPTER XXI

"For you!"

I found that a place had been allotted to me about half-way down the captain's table, on the right-hand side. My immediate neighbors were an Englishman, on his way to the States to buy some commodity in which he dealt, and a very old lady, quite deaf, in charge of a spinster daughter. Neither of them imposed upon me the necessity for conversation. I had, therefore, plenty of time to look around me, and take note of the people in whom I was interested.

They were all seated together, at a small table in the far corner of the saloon. At the head of that table was a man whom I had not yet seen, but whom I at once knew to be Mr. de Valentin. He was tall, rather sallow, with a pointed, black beard, and he continually wore an eyeglass, set in a horn rim, with a narrow, black ribbon. On his right was the woman to whom Adèle had spoken upon the stairs. She wore a plain but elegant dinner-gown of some dark material. She was exquisitely coiffured, and obviously turned out by a perfectly trained maid. There were two girls at the table, whom I judged to be her daughters, and—Adèle.

Adèle was seated so that I could see only her profile. I noticed, however, that she seemed to be eating little, and to be taking but a very small part in the conversation. Once or twice she leaned back in her chair, and looked round the saloon as though in search of some one. On the last of these occasions our eyes met, and she smiled slightly. Mrs. Van Reinberg, who was sitting opposite to her, leaned forward and asked some question. I judged that it concerned me, for immediately afterwards that lady herself raised her gold eyeglass, and favored me with a somewhat deliberate stare. Then she leaned forward again and made some remark to Adèle, the purport of which I could not guess.

Dinner lasted a long time, but I was all the while interested. I was facing Adèle and her friends, so I could observe them all the time without being myself conspicuous. I was able to take note of the somewhat wearied graciousness of Mr. de Valentin, who seemed always to be struggling with a profound boredom; the almost feverish amiability of Mrs. Van Reinberg, and, in a lesser degree, her daughters; and the undoubted reserve with which Adèle seemed to protect herself from Mr. de Valentin's attentions. When at last they rose and left the saloon, I quickly followed their example.

I put on an ulster, lit a cigar, and went up on deck. I found my chair on the sheltered side of the ship, and wrapping myself in a rug, prepared to spend a comfortable half-hour. But I had scarcely settled down before a little group of people came along the deck and halted close to me. A smooth-faced manservant, laden with a pile of magnificent rugs, struck a match and began to examine the labels on the chairs. Its flickering light was apparently sufficient for Adèle to recognize my features.

"So you are going to join the fresh-air brigade, Mr. Courage," she remarked. "I think you are very wise. We found the music-room insufferable."

"I can assure you that the smoke-room is worse, Miss Van Hoyt," I answered, struggling to my feet. "Can I find your chair for you?"

"Thanks, the deck steward is bringing it," she answered. "Let me introduce you to my friends—Mrs. Van Reinberg—my stepmother, Miss Van Reinberg, Miss Sara Van Reinberg, Mr. de Valentin—Mr. Hardross Courage."

I bowed collectively. Mr. de Valentin greeted me stiffly, Mrs. Van Reinberg and the Misses Van Reinberg, with a cordiality which somewhat surprised me.

"I met your cousin, Sir Gilbert, in London, I think, Mr. Courage," she remarked. "He was kind enough to give us tea on the terrace at the House of Commons."

I bowed.

"Gilbert is rather fond of entertaining his friends there," I remarked. "It is the one form of frivolity which seems to appeal to him."

"He was very kind," she continued. "He introduced a number of interesting people to us. The Duke of Westlingham is a relation of yours, is he not?"

"My second cousin," I remarked.

"Is this your first visit to America?" she asked.

"I was once in Canada," I answered. "I have never been in the States."

She smiled at me a little curiously. All the time I felt somehow that she was taking very careful note of my answers.

"We say in my country, you know," she remarked, "that you Englishmen come to us for one of two things only—sport or a wife!"

"I hope to get some of the former, at any rate," I answered. "As for the latter!"

"Well?"

"I have always thought of myself as a bachelor," I said; "but one's good fortune comes sometimes when one least expects it."

I looked across at Adèle, and Mrs. Van Reinberg followed the direction of my eyes. She laughed shrilly, but she did not seem displeased.

116

"If you Englishmen only made as good husbands as you do acquaintances," she said, "I should settle down in London with my girls and study matchmaking. I am afraid, though, that you have your drawbacks."

"Tell me what they are," I begged, "and I will do my best to prove myself an exception."

"You have too much spare time," she declared. "And you know what that leads to?"

"Mr. Courage has not," Adèle interrupted. "He works really very hard indeed."

"Works!" Mrs. Van Reinberg repeated incredulously.

"At games!" Adèle declared. "He plays in cricket matches that last three days long. I saw him once at Lord's, and I can assure you that it looked like very hard work indeed."

Mrs. Van Reinberg turned away with a laugh, and settled herself down into the little nest of rugs which her maid had prepared.

"You young people can walk about, if you like," she said. "I am going to be comfortable. My cigarette case, Annette, and electric lamp. I shall read for half an hour."

She dismissed us all. Adèle and I moved away as though by common consent. Mr. de Valentin followed with the two other girls, though I had noticed that his first impulse had been to take possession of Adèle. She avoided the others skilfully, however, and we strolled off to the farther end of the ship.

"Your stepmother," I remarked, "seems to be a very amiable person!"

"She can be anything she likes," Adèle answered—"upon occasions."

We turned on to the weather side of the ship, which was almost deserted. Adèle glanced behind. Mr. de Valentin and the two girls were still within a few feet of us.

"Do you mind walking on the lower deck?" she asked. "I want to talk to you, and I am sure that we shall be disturbed here."

"With pleasure!" I answered quickly. "I, too, have something to say to you."

We descended in silence to the promenade deck. Here we had the place almost to ourselves. Adèle did not beat about the bush.

117

"Mr. Courage," she said, "tell me what you thought when you saw me on this steamer!"

She looked me full in the face. Her beautiful eyes were full of anxiety. There was about her manner a nervousness which I had never before noticed. Her cheeks were paler, and with these indications of emotion, something of the mystery which had seemed to me always to cling to her personality had departed. She was more natural—more lovable.

"I thought," I answered, "that it was part of the game!—that you were here to watch me. Isn't that the natural conclusion?"

"Mr. Courage," she said, "please look at me."

I faced her at once. Her eyes were fixed upon mine.

"I am not here to watch you," she said quietly. "I came because I have decided to go back to my home in America, and live there quietly for a time. Whatever share I had in the events which led to Leslie Guest's death, these things do not interest me any more. I have finished."

"I congratulate you," I answered.

"I cannot tell you anything about those events, or my connection with them," she went on, "but I want you to believe that I have no longer any association with those who planned them. I am not here to spy upon you. I am not in communication with any one to whom your actions are of any interest. Will you believe this?"

I hesitated for a moment. Her eyes held mine. It was not possible for me to disbelieve her.

"I am glad to hear this," I said seriously.

"You do not doubt me?"

"I cannot," I answered.

She drew a little sigh of relief.

"And now," she said, "about yourself. Be as frank with me as I have been with you. Are you really the legatee of Guest's secret?"

"You know that he told me certain things—before he died," I answered slowly.

118

"Yes! But what are you going to do with the knowledge? Are you going to be wise and let fate take its course, or are you going to meddle in affairs which you know nothing about? Don't do it, Mr. Courage!" she exclaimed, with a sudden catch in her voice. "Leslie Guest was a diplomatist and a schemer all his life, and you know the penalty he paid. You have not the training or the disposition for this sort of thing. You would be foredoomed to failure. Don't do it!"

I turned and looked at her. She was so much in earnest that her whole expression was transformed. The mysterious smile which was so often upon her lips, half supercilious, half mocking, was gone, and with it something of that elusiveness which had so often puzzled me! Her eyes met mine frankly and pleadingly, her fingers were upon my arm, and she was swaying a little towards me with the motion of the boat, so that I was tempted almost beyond measure to take her into my arms, and, with my lips upon hers, promise whatever she would have had me promise. It was only a moment of madness. The memory of other things came back to me.

"It is very good of you," I said slowly, "to warn me. I know that I am not made of the stuff that Guest was. It is possible that I may—"

"It is true, then," she interrupted breathlessly, "you are really meaning to go with his schemes?"

"You take too much for granted," I answered.

"Oh! don't let us misunderstand one another," she begged. "Tell me why you are on your way to America! Tell me why you are on this steamer, of all others."

"I am going to shoot—out West," I said, "and I want to know something of your wonderful country-people!"

She let her fingers slip from my arm.

"You will tell me no more than that," she murmured.

"I have nothing more to tell you," I answered.

Once more she leaned towards me. The wind was blowing around us, she came closer as though seeking for the shelter of my body. I could smell the crushed violets, which she was still wearing at her bosom; her eyes were soft and bright, her lips were slightly parted. I took her into my arms—she clung to me for a moment—one long, delicious moment.

"I have given it all up," she whispered, "for you! If I had told the truth, if I had told them that you knew, it would have meant death! You must forget, you must swear to forget."

119

I held her tightly.

"Dear Adèle," I whispered, "you are a woman who understands. Life and death come to all of us, but a coward could never deserve your love—you could never stoop to care for a man who thought of his life before his honor."

"You are pledged!" she cried.

"I must do what I can," I answered.

She staggered away from me.

"God help us both!" she murmured.

I would have caught her to me again, but a dark figure was coming slowly down the deck. A little, yapping bark came from the deck at her feet. Nagaski was leaping up at his mistress. She stooped and picked him up. He showed me his teeth and snarled.

"You really must make friends with Nagaski, Mr. Courage," she remarked, turning away. "Come, we must go back to the others! My stepmother will think that I am lost."

CHAPTER XXII

"*Loved* I *not honor more*"

I told Guest exactly what had passed between Adèle and myself, leaving out only the personal element, at which I allowed him to guess. He was thoughtful for some time afterwards.

"What is to be the end of it between you and her?" he asked me presently. "Exactly on what terms do you stand at present?"

"Some day," I answered, "I shall marry her—or no other woman. As regards other matters, I believe that she is neutral."

"You do not think, then, that she will obstruct our plans?" he asked. "Of course, a word from her, and our journey to America can only end in failure."

"She will not speak it," I answered confidently. "I do not know, of course, how deeply she was involved in the schemes of those whom we may call our enemies, but I am perfectly certain that she has finished with them now."

Guest nodded.

"I hope so," he remarked shortly. "At any rate, it is one of the risks which we must take."

We said no more about the subject then, and I very soon perceived that the intimacy between Adèle and myself was likely to be of the greatest use to us. For the next two days neither of us referred to those things which lay in the background. We walked and sat together, played shuffleboard, and in every way made the most of all those delightful opportunities of *tête-à-têtes* which a sea voyage affords. Mrs. Van Reinberg, for some reason or other, watched our intimacy with increasing satisfaction. Mr. de Valentin, on the other hand, though he concealed his feelings admirably, seemed to find it equally distasteful. Gradually the situation became clear to me. Mrs. Van Reinberg desired to reserve the whole interest of Mr. de Valentin for herself and her daughters; he, on the other hand, had shown signs of a partiality for Adèle. The fates were certainly working for me.

On the third night out we were all together on deck after dinner. I was standing near Mrs. Van Reinberg, who had been exceedingly gracious to me.

"Tell me, Mr. Courage," she asked, "what are your plans when you land?"

"I thought of using some of my letters of introduction," I answered, "and going West after Christmas. I have been told that the country round Lenox and Pittsfield is very beautiful just now, and I shall stay, I expect, with a man I know fairly well, who lives up there—Plaskett White."

"Why, isn't that strange?" Mrs. Van Reinberg exclaimed. "The Plaskett Whites are our nearest neighbors. If you really are coming that way, you must stay with us for a week, or as long as you can manage it. We are going straight to Lenox."

"I shall be delighted," I answered heartily.

Mr. de Valentin dropped his eyeglass and polished it deliberately. His usually expressionless face was black with anger. Even the two girls looked a little surprised at their mother's invitation. I felt that the situation was a delicate one.

"I should not be able to intrude upon you for more than a day or two," I remarked, a little diffidently, "but if you will really put me up for that length of time, I shall look forward to my visit with a great deal of pleasure."

Mrs. Van Reinberg was looking across at Mr. de Valentin with a very determined expression on her pale, hard face. She was obviously a woman who was accustomed to have her own way, and meant to have it in this particular instance.

"It is settled, then, Mr. Courage," she declared. "Come whenever you like. We can always make room for you."

I bowed my gratitude, and, to relieve the situation, I took Adèle away with me for a walk. We were scarcely out of hearing, before I heard Mr. de Valentin's cold but angry voice.

"My dear Madame, do you consider that invitation of yours a prudent one? ..."

We walked on the other side of the deck. Adèle was silent for several moments. Then she turned towards me, and the old smile was upon her lips—the smile which had always half fascinated, half irritated me.

"So," she remarked, "I have become your unwilling ally."

"In what way?" I asked.

"I suppose," she said, "that an invitation to Lenox *was* necessary to your plans, wasn't it?"

"I had fairly obvious reasons for hoping for one," I answered, smiling.

She passed her arm through mine, and leaned a little towards me. It was at such moments that I found her so dangerously sweet.

"Ah!" she murmured, "I wish that that were the only reason!"

I pressed her arm to mine, but I said nothing. When I could avoid it, I preferred not to discuss those other matters. We walked to the ship's side, and leaned over to watch the phosphorus. Suddenly she whispered in my ear, her lips were so close to my cheek that I felt her warm breath.

"Jim," she said, "do you love me very much?"

I would have kissed the lips which dared to ask such a question, but she drew a little away. It was not that which she wanted—just then.

"Listen," she murmured, "but do not look at me. Watch that star there, sinking down towards the sea—there near the horizon. Now listen. When we land at New York, let us run away from everything, from everybody. We can go west to Mexico and beyond! There are beautiful countries there which I have always wanted to see. Let us lose ourselves for a year, two years—longer even. I will not let you be weary! Oh! I promise you that. I will give you myself and all my life. Think! We can only live once, and you and I have found what life is. Don't let us trifle with it. Jim, will you come?"

Soft though her voice was, there was passion quivering in every sentence. When I turned to look at her, her eyes and face seemed aflame with it. The color had streamed into her cheeks, she had drifted into my arms, and her clinging lips yielded unresistingly to mine.

"Oh! Jim," she murmured, "the rest isn't worth anything. Tell me that you will come."

I did not answer her at once, and she seemed content to lie where she was. My own senses were in a wild tumult of delight, but there was a pain in my heart. Presently she drew a little away. There was a new note in her tone—a note of half-alarmed surprise.

"Answer me, Jim! Oh! answer me please," she begged. "Don't let me think—that you mean to refuse."

I held her tightly in my arms. The memory of that moment might have to last me all my life.

"My dear heart," I whispered, "it would be Paradise! Some day we will do it. But in your heart, you know very well that you would love me no more if I forgot my honor and my duty—even for the love of you!"

"It is not your task," she pleaded. "Tell what you know, and leave it to others. You are too honest to play the spy. You will fail, and it will cost you your life."

"I shall not fail," I answered steadfastly, "and my life is insured in Heaven for the sake of the things I carry with me. Have faith in me, Adèle. I swear that I will do my duty and live to realize—everything."

She shook her head sadly.

"There are others," she said, "who could do what you are doing. But for me there is no one else in the world."

"You shall not need any one else," I declared. "Mine is, after all, a simple task. You know that I went to see Lord Polloch in London."

"Well?"

"He would not believe me. Why should he? My story sounded wild enough, and I had no proofs. I only need to gather together a few of these loose ends, to weave something tangible out of them and show him the results, and my task is finished."

"Do you suppose," she asked quietly, "that you will be allowed to do that?"

"I must do my best,"' I answered. "It is inevitable. There will be more Mr. Stanleys and such like, no doubt. They may hinder me, but I think that, in the end, I shall pull through. And I promise you, dear, that when I have something definite to show, I shall have finished with the whole business. It is no more to my liking than yours."

"I cannot move you then," she murmured.

"You must not try," I answered.

She laughed a little unnaturally.

"I do not feel any longer," she said, "that you belong to me. There is something else which comes first."

"Without that something, dear," I answered, "I should not be worthy of your love."

"With men, there is always something else," she said sadly. "It is the woman only who realizes what love is, who puts it before body and soul and honor. A man cannot do that."

"No!" I answered softly, "a man cannot do that."

She turned away, and I walked by her side in silence. When she reached the companion-way, she stepped inside a little abruptly.

124

"I am going to my state-room," she said. "Good night!"

"You are not angry with me, Adèle?" I asked anxiously.

"No! not that," she answered. "Of course, you are right. Only I have been a little mad, and I dreamed a beautiful dream. It is all impossible, of course; but I don't feel like bridge or my stepmother's questions. Say I am coming up again. It will save trouble!"

I played bridge later with Mrs. Van Reinberg for a partner. Mr. de Valentin's manner to me was coldly frigid, and a general air of restraint seemed to indicate that the evening had scarcely been a cheerful one. I myself did not feel much like contributing towards a more hilarious state of affairs. We had one rubber only, and then Mrs. Van Reinberg, who as a rule hated to go to bed before midnight, announced her intention of retiring. She accepted my escort to the door, and bade Mr. de Valentin a cold good-night.

"I hope you will understand, Mr. Courage," she said, as we shook hands, "that I shall expect you at Lenox. You won't disappoint us?"

"There isn't the faintest chance that I shall do so, Mrs. Van Reinberg," I answered. "I have the best of reasons for wishing to come."

She smiled at me encouragingly.

"May I guess at the attraction?" she asked.

"I fancy," I answered, "that it is fairly apparent. May I, by the way, Mrs. Van Reinberg," I continued, "ask you a question?"

"Certainly," she answered.

"It is rather a delicate matter to allude to," I said; "but your friend, Mr. de Valentin, seemed to find your invitation to me a matter for personal disapproval. I hope that I have not unwillingly been the cause of any unpleasantness?"

Mrs. Van Reinberg was a little embarrassed. She hesitated, and dropped her voice a little in answering me.

"Since you have mentioned it, Mr. Courage," she said, "I will treat you confidentially. Mr. de Valentin has shown a desire to become an admirer of my stepdaughter. For several reasons, I find it necessary to discourage his advances. In fact, between ourselves, Mr. de Valentin, although he is a person for whom I have a great respect and esteem, would be an altogether impossible suitor for Adèle. I am sure he will realize that directly he thinks the matter over seriously; but you see he is a person who has been very much spoilt, and he annoyed me to-night very much. I do not care to have my invitations criticised by my other guests, whoever they may be. Now you understand the position, Mr. Courage."

"Perfectly," I answered. "I am exceedingly obliged to you for being so frank with me."

"And we shall expect you at Lenox?"

"Without fail!" I answered confidently.

She passed down the stairs, humming a tune to herself, followed a few steps behind by her maid. Her wonderfully arranged, fair hair was ablaze with diamonds, her gown was more suitable to a London drawing-room than the deck of a steamer. And yet she seemed neither over-jewelled nor over-dressed. She had all the marvellous "aplomb" of her countrywomen, who can transgress all laws of fashion or taste, and through sheer self-confidence remain correct.

I felt a touch upon my shoulder and turned around. It was Mr. de Valentin who stood there.

"I beg your pardon, Mr. Courage," he said, "but if you have nothing particular to do for a few minutes, will you smoke a cigarette with me?"

"With pleasure!" I answered. "I was just going into the smoke-room."

He stalked solemnly ahead, and I followed him along the corridor.

CHAPTER XXIII

THE PRETENDER

Mr. de Valentin led the way to a secluded corner of the smoke-room, and laid a well-filled cigarette case upon the table. He beckoned to the steward.

"You will take something?" he asked.

I ordered a whisky and soda and lit a cigarette. I had tasted nothing like them since I had left England. Mr. de Valentin leaned across the table towards me.

"Mr. Courage," he said, "I am going to ask you to accept a confidence from me. You are an English gentleman, and although I have not the honor to be myself an Englishman, my associations with your country have always been very close, and I am well aware that a special significance attaches itself to that term."

He paused and looked across at me somewhat anxiously. His speech was slow but very distinct. He had little accent, but I had known quite well that he was not an Englishman.

"I shall be very glad to hear anything that you have to say, Mr. de Valentin," I answered.

He beat with his forefinger upon the table for a few moments absently. I found myself studying him critically. His appearance was without doubt distinguished. His sallow face, his pointed black beard, his high, well-shaped nose, and almost brilliant eyes gave him the appearance of a Spaniard; but the scrupulous exactness of his plain dinner clothes, his well-manicured nails, and the ring upon his little finger, with its wonderful green stone, were all suggestive of the French aristocrat. His eyebrows were knit just now, as though with thought. Presently he looked up from the table and continued:

"If you will permit me," he said, "I should like to introduce myself. My name is not Mr. de Valentin. I am Victor Louis, Comte de Valentin, Marquis de St. Auteuil, Duc de Bordera and Escault, Prince of Normandy."

I nodded gravely.

"And according to some," I remarked in a low tone, "King of France!"

He looked at me in keen surprise. He was evidently taken aback.

"You knew me?" he exclaimed.

"I felt very sure," I answered, "that you were the person whom you have declared yourself to be. I have seen you twice in Paris, and you must remember that this is an age of illustrated papers and journalistic enterprise."

"You have not mentioned your recognition of me?" he asked quickly.

"Certainly not," I answered. "It was not my affair, and in your position I can conceive that there may be many reasons for your desiring to travel incognito."

He smiled a little wearily.

"Yet it would tax your ingenuity, I imagine," he continued, "to account for my travelling in company with Mrs. Van Reinberg and her daughters."

"It is not my affair," I answered. "We Englishmen are supposed to have learnt the secret of minding our own business."

"You Englishmen, certainly," he answered, "but not always your servants."

I looked at him a little puzzled. His words had seemed to possess some special significance.

"You will not, I am sure, take offence at what I am about to say, Mr. Courage," he continued; "but may I ask if you have confidence in the manservant who is now travelling with you?"

It was a shock, but I fancy that I remained unmoved.

"You mean my man Peters?" I inquired. "I can guarantee his honesty certainly."

"Can you also guarantee," Mr. de Valentin asked me, "that he is simply what he professes to be—a valet, and not, for instance, a spy?"

"My dear sir," I protested, "we scarcely know the meaning of that word in England. To say the least of it, such a suggestion would be wildly improbable."

He sighed.

"In France," he said, "one looks for spies everywhere. I myself have suffered painfully on more than one occasion from espionage. One grows suspicious, and, in this instance, I have grounds for my suspicions."

"May I know what they are?" I asked.

"I was about to tell you," Mr. de Valentin answered. "I have with me in my cabin certain papers, which are of great importance to me. I had occasion to look them through last night, and although none were missing, yet there was every indication of their having been tampered with. I questioned my servant, who is a very faithful fellow, and I found that the only person with whom he had made friends, and who had entered my cabin, was your man, Peters I think you called him."

Mr. de Valentin was watching me closely, and the test was a severe one. I was annoyed with Guest for having kept me in ignorance of what he had done.

"I do not see how your private papers could have been of the slightest use to Peters," I said; "but if you like to come down to my state-room you can question him yourself."

"That," he answered, "I will leave to you. I take it then that you have no suspicion that your servant is any other than he professes to be?"

"I am perfectly convinced that he is not," I declared.

Mr. de Valentin bowed.

"For the moment," he said, "we will quit the subject. I have another matter, equally delicate, which I should like to discuss with you."

"I am quite at your service," I assured him.

"You have a saying in English," he continued, "which, if I remember it rightly, says that necessity makes strange bedfellows. I myself am going into a strange country upon a strange errand. I do not consider myself a person of hyper-exclusive tastes, but I must confess that I do not find myself in sympathy with the country-people and friends of Mrs. Van Reinberg!"

I shrugged my shoulders.

"Then why go amongst them?" I asked. "You are surely at liberty to do as you choose!"

Mr. de Valentin took up his case and chose another cigarette.

"In this instance," he said coldly, "I am not entirely my own master. There were powerful reasons why I should have taken this voyage to America, and there are reasons why I should have done so with Mrs. Van Reinberg. Which brings me, by the bye, to the second matter concerning which I wished to speak to you."

I accepted another of Mr. de Valentin's excellent cigarettes, and composed myself once more to listen.

"I am going to Lenox," he continued, "to meet there a few American friends, with whom I have certain affairs of importance to discuss. You, also, have been invited to Lenox. My request is that you defer your visit there until after my departure."

I raised my eyebrows at this. It seemed to me that Mr. de Valentin was going a little too far.

"May I inquire," I asked politely, "in what respect you find my presence there undesirable? We are not bound, I presume, to come much into contact with one another."

"You misunderstand me," Mr. de Valentin declared. "It is not a personal matter at all. My visit to Lenox has been arranged solely to discuss a certain matter with certain people. The presence of those who are not interested in it would be an embarrassment to all of us. Further, to recur to a matter which we have already spoken of, I cannot divest myself of certain suspicions concerning your servant."

I considered my reply for a moment or two.

"As regards the latter," I said after a pause, "I can not take you seriously. Besides, it is very unlikely that my servant would accompany me to Lenox. If my presence there would be an embarrassment, I really do not see why Mrs. Van Reinberg asked me."

"She did so thoughtlessly," Mr. de Valentin answered. "Her reasons were tolerably clear to me, perhaps to you. With regard to them, I have nothing to say, except that your visit could be paid just as well, say in a fortnight after we land."

"Unfortunately," I answered, "that would not suit me. To be frank with you, Miss Van Hoyt would have left."

"If I can arrange," Mr. de Valentin continued, with some eagerness, "that she should not have left!"

I hesitated for a moment.

"Mr. de Valentin," I said, "I cannot conceive what cause for embarrassment could arise from my presence in Lenox at the same time as yourself. I do not ask you to tell me your secrets; but, in the absence of some more valid reason for staying away, I shall certainly not break my present engagement."

There was a silence between us for several moments. Mr. de Valentin was fingering his cigarette case nervously.

"I am perhaps asking too much of a stranger, Mr. Courage," he said. "The matter is of the deepest importance to me, or I would not have troubled you. Supposing Miss Van Hoyt should herself fix the date of your visit, and engage to be there?"

"That," I answered, "would, of course, be sufficient for me."

Mr. de Valentin rose from his seat.

"We will leave it like that then," he said. "I must apologize, Mr. Courage, for having troubled you with my private affairs, and wish you good-night!"

We separated a few moments later, and I went down to my state-room. I found Guest busy writing in a pocket-book, seated on the edge of his bunk. I told him of my conversation with Mr. de Valentin.

"I knew it was risky," he remarked when I had finished, "but it was an opportunity which I dared not miss."

"You might have told me about it," I protested. "I was altogether unprepared."

"The less you know," he answered, "the better. If you like, I will show you tracings of some letters which I discovered in Mr. de Valentin's portfolio. They were quite worth the journey to America, apart from anything else. Personally, I should advise you not to see them until our return to England."

"Very well," I answered. "Don't show them to me. But I shouldn't try it again. Mr. de Valentin is on his guard."

Guest smiled a little wearily.

"I am not likely to make such a mistake as that," he answered. "Besides, I have been through all his papers. His secrets are ours now, only we must know what is decided upon at Lenox. Then we can return to England, and the first part of our task will be done!"

CHAPTER XXIV

A PRACTICAL WOMAN

Mrs. Van Reinberg on the steamer was a somewhat formidable person; Mrs. Van Reinberg in her own house was despotism personified. Her word was law, her rule was absolute. Consequently, when she swept out on to the sunny piazza, where a little party of us were busy discussing our plans for the day, we all turned towards her expectantly. We might propose, but Mrs. Van Reinberg would surely dispose. We waited to hear what she might have to say.

"I want to talk to Mr. Courage," she declared. "All the rest of you go away!"

They obeyed her at once. We were alone in less than a minute. Mrs. Van Reinberg established herself in a low wicker chair, and I took up my position within a few feet of her, leaning against the wooden rail.

"I am entirely at your service, Mrs. Van Reinberg," I declared. "What is it to be about—Adèle?"

"No! not Adèle," she answered. "I leave you and Adèle to arrange your own affairs. You can manage that without any interference from me."

I smiled and waited for her to proceed. She was evidently thinking out her way. Her brows were knitted, her eyes were fixed upon a distant spot in the forest landscape of orange and red. Yet I was very sure that at that moment, the wonderful autumnal tints, which she seemed to be so steadily regarding, held no place in her thoughts.

"Mr. Courage," she said at last, "you are a sensible man, and a man of honor. I should like to talk to you confidentially."

I murmured something about being flattered, but I do not think that she heard me.

"I should like," she continued, "to have you understand certain things which are in my mind just now, and which concern also—Mr. de Valentin."

I nodded. The Prince's identity was an open secret, but his incognito was jealously observed.

"I wonder," she said slowly, looking for the first time directly towards me, "whether you have ever seriously considered the question of the American woman—such as myself, for instance!"

I was a little puzzled, and no doubt I looked it. Mrs. Van Reinberg proceeded calmly. It was made clear to me that, for the present, at any rate, my rôle was to be simply that of listener.

"My own case," she said, "is typical. At least I suppose so! I speak for myself; and there are others in the house, at the present moment, who profess to feel as I do, and suffer—as I have done. In this country, we are taught that wealth is power. We, or rather our husbands, acquire or inherit it; afterwards we set ourselves to test the truth of that little maxim. We begin at home. In about three years, more or less, we reach our limitations. Then it begins to dawn upon us that, whatever else America is good for, it's no place for a woman with ambitions. We're on the top too soon, and when we're there it doesn't amount to anything."

"Which accounts," I remarked, "for the invasion of Europe!"

Mrs. Van Reinberg leaned her fair, little head upon her white be-ringed fingers, and looked steadily at me. I had never for a moment under-estimated her, but she had probably never so much impressed me. There was something Napoleonic about this slow unfolding of her carefully thought-out plans.

"Naturally," she answered. "What, however, so few of us are able to realize is our utter and miserable failure in what you are pleased to call that invasion."

"Failure!" I repeated incredulously. "I do not understand that. One hears everywhere of the social triumphs of the American woman."

Mrs. Van Reinberg's eyes shone straight into mine. Her face expressed the most unmitigated contempt.

"Social triumphs!" she repeated scornfully. "What clap-trap! I tell you that a season in London or Paris, much more Vienna, is enough to drive a real American woman crazy. Success, indeed! What does it amount to?"

She paused for a moment to take breath. I realized then that the woman whom I had known was something of a fraud, a puppet hung out with the rags of a European manner, according to the study and observation of the shrewd, little lady who pulled the strings. It was Mrs. Van Reinberg of London and Paris whom I had met upon the steamer; it was Mrs. Van Reinberg of New York who was talking to me now, and she was speaking in her own language.

"Look here, Mr. Courage," she said, leaning towards me with her elbows upon her knees, and nothing left of that elegant pose which she had at first assumed. "I suppose I've got my full share of the American spirit, and I tell you I'm a bad hand at taking a back seat anywhere, or even a front one on sufferance. And yet, wherever we go in Europe, that's what we've got to put up with! You think we're mad on titles over here! We aren't, but we are keen on what a title brings over your side.

Take your Debrett—there are I don't know how many baronets and lords and marquises and earls, and all the rest of it. Do you realize that whatever public place I'm in, or even at a friend's dinner-party, the homely, stupid wives of those men have got to go in before me, and if they don't—why I know all the time it's a matter of courtesy? That's what makes me mad! Don't you dare to smile at me now. I'm in deadly earnest. In this country, so far as society goes, I'm at the top. You may say it doesn't amount to much, and you're right. But it makes it all the worse when I'm in Europe, and see the sort of women I have to give place to. Say, don't you sit there, Mr. Courage, and look at me as though I were a woman with some cranky grievance to talk about. It's got beyond that, let me tell you!"

"I can assure you, Mrs. Van Reinberg—" I began.

"Now listen here, Mr. Courage," she interrupted. "I'm not the sort of woman to complain at what I don't try to alter. What's the good of having a husband whose nod is supposed to shake the money markets of the world, if you don't make use of him?"

I nodded sagely.

"You are quite right," I said. "Money, after all, is the greatest power in the world to-day. Money will buy anything!"

"I guess so, if it's properly spent," Mrs. Van Reinberg agreed. "Only very few of my country-people have any idea how to use it to get what they want. They go over the other side and hire great houses, and bribe your great ladies to call themselves their friends, and bribe your young men with wonderful entertainments to come to their houses. They spend, spend, spend, and think they are getting value for their money. Idiots! The great lady whom they are proud to entertain one night is as likely as not to cut them the next. Half the people who go to their parties go out of curiosity, and half to meet their own friends. Not one to see them! Not one because it does them the slightest good to be seen there. They are there in the midst of it all, and that is all you can say. Their motto should be 'on sufferance.' That's what I call going to work the wrong way."

"You have," I suggested, "some other scheme?"

She drew her chair a little closer to mine, and looked around cautiously.

"I have," she admitted. "That is what we are all here for—to discuss it and make our final plans."

"And Prince Victor?" I murmured.

"Precisely! He is in it, of course. I may as well tell you that he's dead against my making a confidant of you; but I've a sort of fancy to hear what you might have to

134

say about it. You see I'm a practical woman, and though I've thought this scheme out myself, and I believe in it, there are times when it seems to me a trifle airy. Now you're a kind of level-headed person, and living over there, your point of view would be interesting."

"I should be glad to hear anything you might have to tell me, Mrs. Van Reinberg," I said slowly; "but you must please remember that I am an Englishman."

"Oh! we don't want to hurt your old country," she declared. "I consider that for all the talk about kinship, and all that sort of thing, she treats us—I mean women like myself—disgracefully. But that's neither here nor there. I've finished with England for the present. We're going to play a greater game than that!"

Mrs. Van Reinberg had dropped her voice a little. There was a somewhat uncomfortable pause. I could see that, even at the last moment, she realized that, in telling me these things, she was guilty of what might well turn out to be a colossal indiscretion. I myself was almost in a worse dilemma. If I accepted her confidence, I was almost, if not quite, bound in honor to respect it. If, as I suspected, it fitted in with the great scheme, if it indeed formed ever so small a part of these impending happenings in which Guest so firmly believed, what measure of respect were we likely to pay to it? None at all! If I stopped her, I should be guilty, from Guest's point of view, of incredible folly; if I let her go on, it must be with the consciousness that I was accepting her confidences under wholly false pretences. It was a big problem for a man like myself, new to the complexities of life. I could only think of Guest's words: "Conscience! For Heaven's sake, man, lock it up until we have done our duty."

I leaned against the wooden rail of the piazza, looking across the grounds. Within a dozen yards or so of us, several of Mrs. Van Reinberg's guests, with a collection of golf sticks, were clambering into a huge automobile. Beyond the pleasure gardens was a range of forest-covered hills, yellow and gold now with the glory of the changing foliage. In the valley was a small steeplechase course, towards which several people were riding. The horse which had been saddled for me was still being led about a little way down the avenue. With the exception that there was no shooting party, it was very much like the usual sort of gathering at an English country house. And yet it all seemed wholly unreal to me! I felt a strong inclination—perhaps a little hysterical—to burst out laughing. This was surely a gigantic joke, planned against the proverbial lack of humor of my countrymen! I was not expected to take it seriously! And yet, in a moment, I remembered certain established facts, of which these things were but the natural sequel. I remembered, too, a certain air of seriousness, and a disposition towards confidential talk, manifested among the older members of the party. Mrs. Van Reinberg's suppressed but earnest voice again broke the silence. She called me back to her side.

"Mr. Courage," she said, "you are going to marry Adèle?"

"I hope so," I answered confidently, glancing away to where she stood talking to Mr. de Valentin on the piazza steps.

"I shall treat you then," she declared, "as one of the family. To-night, after dinner, we are going to hold the meeting for which this houseful of people was really brought together. I invite you to come to it. Afterwards you will understand everything! Now I must hurry off, and so must you! Your horse is getting the fidgets."

She swept off down the piazza. Mr. de Valentin came forward eagerly to meet her. I saw his face darken as she whispered in his ear.

CHAPTER XXV

A CABLE FROM EUROPE

Dinner that night was a somewhat oppressive meal. Several new guests had arrived, some of whom bore names which were well known to me. There was a sense of some hidden excitement, which formed an uneasy background to the spasmodic general conversation. The men especially seemed uncomfortable and ill at ease.

"Poor father," Adèle whispered to me, "he would give a good many of his dollars not to be in this."

I glanced across at our host, who had come down from New York specially in his magnificent private car, which was now awaiting his return on a siding of the little station. He was a hard-faced, elderly man, with a shrewd mouth and keen eyes, sparely built, yet a man you would be inclined to glance at twice in any assemblage. He wore a most unconventional evening suit, the waistcoat cut very high, and a plain black tie. Two footmen stood behind his chair, and a large florid lady, wearing a crown of diamonds, and with a European reputation for opulence, sat on his right hand. Neither seemed to embarrass him in the least, for the simple reason that he took no notice of them. He drank water, ate sparingly, and talked Wall Street with a man a few places down the table on the left. His speech was crisp and correct, but his intonation more distinctly American than any of his guests'. On the whole, I think he interested me more than any one else there.

"By the bye," I remarked, "I ought to be having a little private conversation with your father this time, oughtn't I?"

She smiled at me faintly.

"It is usual," she assented. "I don't think you will find that he will have much to say. I am my own mistress, and he is too wise to interfere in such a matter. But—"

"Well?"

"You are a very confident person," she murmured.

"I am confident of one thing, at any rate," I answered, "and that is that you are going to be my wife!"

She rebuked me with a glance, which was also wonderfully sweet.

"Some one will hear you," she whispered.

I shook my head.

"Every one is too busy talking about the mysteries to come," I declared.

She shrugged her dazzlingly white shoulders.

"Perhaps even you," she murmured, "may take them more seriously some day."

A few minutes later Mrs. Van Reinberg rose.

"We shall all meet," she remarked, looking round the table, "at eleven o'clock in the library."

In common with most of the younger men, I left the table at the same time, the usual custom, I had discovered, here, where cigarettes were smoked indiscriminately. There was baccarat in the hall; billiards and bridge for those who care for them. Mrs. Van Reinberg waited for me in the first of the long suite of reception-rooms. Mr. de Valentin, who had been talking earnestly to her most of the time during the service of dinner, remained only a few paces off. It struck me that Mrs. Van Reinberg was not in the best of humors.

"Mr. Courage," she said, "I think it only right that I should let you know that Mr. de Valentin strongly objects to your presence at our meeting to-night."

"I am very sorry to hear it," I answered. "May I ask upon what grounds?"

"He seems to imagine," she declared, "that you are not trustworthy."

Mr. de Valentin hastily intervened.

"My dear Mrs. Van Reinberg!" he exclaimed.

"I hope you will believe, Mr. Courage," he continued, turning towards me, "that nothing was further from my thoughts. I simply say that as you are not interested in the matter which we are going to discuss, your presence is quite unnecessary, and might become a source of mutual embarrassment."

"On the contrary," I assured him, "I am very much interested. Perhaps Mr. de Valentin does not know," I added, turning towards Mrs. Van Reinberg, "that your stepdaughter has done me the honor of promising to be my wife."

There was a moment's breathless pause. I saw Mrs. Van Reinberg falter, and I saw something which I did not understand flash across Mr. de Valentin's face.

"Even in that case," he said in a very low tone, "Miss Van Hoyt will herself be present. It is not necessary that you should accompany her."

138

"I regret to say that I think differently," I answered. "Unless Mrs. Van Reinberg withdraws her invitation, I shall certainly be present."

"That," Mrs. Van Reinberg declared, "I shall not do. Mr. Courage must do as he thinks best."

Mr. de Valentin bowed slightly, and turned away. His lips were parted in a very unpleasant and most peculiar smile.

"I am very sorry," I said to Mrs. Van Reinberg, "to be the cause of any uneasiness."

"The Prince," she answered, departing for the first time from the use of his incognito, "is very nervous. He is used to advisers and friends, and, for almost the first time in his life, he is entirely alone. I sometimes wonder whether he has really sufficient nerve to take up a great part in life."

"Circumstances," I remarked, "often create the man!"

"I hope," she said a little grimly, "that they will make a man of Mr. de Valentin."

She took a cigarette from the little gold case which hung from her chatelaine, and lit it.

"I will tell you, Mr. Courage," she said, "why I am rather anxious for you to be present at the meeting to-night. You are altogether disinterested, and you should be able to form a sane opinion of Mr. de Valentin's proposals. I should like to hear how they appeal to you."

I bowed.

"I will tell you exactly what I think," I answered.

She dismissed me with a little nod.

I went in search of Adèle, but could find no trace of her in any of the rooms. At last, in one of the corridors, I heard Nagaski barking, and found him sitting outside the closed door of a small reading-room. Directly I moved towards him, however, he flew at me, and seized my trousers between his teeth. His eyes were fierce with anger, his whole skin seemed to be quivering with excitement. At the sound of his angry growls, the door was opened, and Adèle appeared.

"Nagaski, you naughty dog!" she exclaimed.

Nagaski let go of my trousers, but continued to growl. Adèle stooped to pick him up, and he immediately attempted to lick her face. I saw then, to my surprise, that she was very pale, and had all the appearance of having received a shock.

"What has happened?" I asked.

She motioned me to enter the room, and closed the door behind us.

"I have just received a cable from Europe," she said in a low tone. "It concerns you!"

I looked at her keenly.

"Well?"

"Something has been found out. A friend of Mr. Stanley's left Havre yesterday for New York. You will not be safe for a moment after he arrives. And in the meantime, I have a message for Mr. de Valentin. I wonder," she added, with a faint smile, "what chance you would have of being at the meeting to-night, if I should deliver it now?"

"Then please don't deliver it," I begged. "I am really getting curious about this affair. You can hold it back for an hour or so, can't you?"

"Yes!" she answered quietly, "I can do that."

She was a changed being during the last hour. Her eyes were full of fear, she seemed to have lost alike her brilliancy and her splendid courage. She did not resist me when I took her into my arms, but her very passiveness was ominous.

"Come," I said cheerfully, "this really isn't so serious as it seems. I shall be away from here before Mr. Stanley's friend arrives, I may even be out of the country. Why shouldn't you come with me, Adèle?"

She disengaged herself gently from my arms.

"You are a very thoughtless person," she said quietly. "Not only would it be impossible for me to do that, but there must not be a word about our engagement. Remember that I have given false information about you. It is not the risk for myself that I mind so much, but—there are other things! To-morrow you or I must leave here!"

"It shall be I, of course," I answered. "I was going anyhow. Don't lose heart, Adèle. If we are to be separated, it shall not be for long!"

She shook her head, but she smiled at me, although it was a little sadly.

"We may not have the power to decide that for ourselves," she answered. "Listen!"

The great clock in the tower over the stables was striking eleven. We listened until it had finished.

"Now kiss me, dear," she said, leaning towards me.

I stooped down, and her arms were suddenly around me like a vise. She clung to me with her whole body, and held me so that I could scarcely breathe.

"I will not let you go," she cried. "It is death for you if you learn their plans. Fate has given you to me, and no one shall take you away. Oh! stay with me, Jim—my sweetheart—my dear! dear! dear!"

Her lips were upon mine before I could speak. She was drawing me away from the door. Her eyes, her arms, her whole body seemed to be pleading with me. Then suddenly there came a low knocking at the door. I stood away—no longer a prisoner. It was a wonderful intervention this! How else could I have escaped?

The door opened slowly. It was the French maid who stood there. She looked around the room and beckoned to the dog.

"I beg mademoiselle's pardon," she said. "I came for Nagaski. I heard him whine, and I thought that he was alone."

She stood there motionless, her pale, expressionless face turned towards us, her full black eyes turned hurriedly away. I think that she knew what she had done. Adèle sank down upon the sofa, and Nagaski, with a low growl at me, sprang into her lap. I left the room ungracefully enough, with only a muttered word of farewell. As I passed along the corridor, I heard Nagaski's bark of joy!

CHAPTER XXVI

FOR VALUE RECEIVED

There were exactly twelve people present when I entered the room and took my place at the long table—six men and six women, Mr. de Valentin sat at the extreme end, and as I entered his face grew dark with sudden anger. He glanced quickly at Mrs. Van Reinberg, who, however, was whispering to her husband, and declined to look. Then he half rose to his feet and addressed me.

"Mr. Courage," he said, "this is a little private gathering between these friends of mine and myself, to discuss a private matter in which we are all much interested. Under these circumstances, I trust that you will not think it discourteous if I ask you to withdraw. Your presence might very possibly tend to check free discussion, and, I might add, would be a source of embarrassment to myself."

I glanced towards Mrs. Van Reinberg.

"I am here," I said, "by the invitation of our hostess. If Mrs. Van Reinberg asks me to withdraw, I should, of course, have no alternative but to do so. I should like to say, however, that it would give me very much pleasure to be admitted to your conference, and any advice I might be able to offer as an impartial person would be entirely at your service."

Mrs. Van Reinberg whispered for a moment with her husband, who then leaned over towards me.

"Mr. Courage," he said, "I believe you to be a person of common sense. I am not sure that I can say the same for the rest of us here. Seems to me I'd like to have you stop; but there is one thing I think should be understood. This is a private meeting of friends. Are you prepared, as a man of honor, to give your word to keep secret whatever passes here?"

I was afraid that some condition of this sort would be imposed, but I was ready with my answer.

"Most certainly I am, Mr. Van Reinberg," I declared, "with one reservation, and that is that nothing is proposed which is inimical to my country. I presume that I may take that for granted?"

"You may," Mr. Van Reinberg answered shortly. "We are not such fools as to run up against the old country. On the contrary, Mr. de Valentin has assured us that his scheme has a little more than the moral support of your government."

Mr. de Valentin intervened with a little gesture of excitement.

"No!" he exclaimed, "I do not. I must not go so far as that. I do not mention any government by name."

"Quite right," Mr. Van Reinberg assented, "but the fact's there all the same. I guess you can stay where you are, Mr. Courage!"

Mr. de Valentin shot an evil glance at me, but he leaned back in his chair with the air of a man who has no more to say. Mr. Van Reinberg, on the other hand, cleared his throat and stood up.

"Well," he said, "we'll get to business. I've a word or two to say first to you, Hickson, and my other friends. We've none of us been idlers in the world. We started out to make money, and we've made it. We're probably worth more than any other five men in the world. We can control the finance of every nation, we can rule the money markets of every capital in Europe. Personally I'm satisfied. I guess you are. It seems, however, that our wives aren't. I'm sorry for it, but it can't be helped. They want something that dollars in the ordinary way can't buy. This scheme is to meet that case. It's my wife's idea—my wife's and Mr. de Valentin's between them. I take it that if you go into it you'll go into it for the same reason that I do—for your wives' sakes. I want to make this clear, for I tell you frankly I think it's the biggest fool's game I've ever taken a hand in. I'm proud of my name, if my wife isn't. If any one got calling me Monsieur le Duc of anything, I guess my fingers 'd itch to knock him down. If our wives, however, won't be happy till they hear themselves called Madame la Duchesse, I suppose we've got to take a back seat. Mr. de Valentin here says that he's the rightful King of France. I know nothing about history, but no doubt he's right. He says, too, that in their hearts the French people want him on the throne, and, with money, he says he could find his way there. The bargain is, I understand, that we find the money, and he establishes our wives well amongst the aristocracy of France. He asks for twelve million dollars, that is two millions each. If my wife asks me to, I shall put my lot down, much as I should buy her the Czar of Russia's crown if it came on the market, and she wanted it. It's for you to say whether you want to come in. If you want to ask any questions, there's Mr. de Valentin. He's come over to fix the thing up, and I guess he's prepared to give you all particulars."

There was a little murmur of conversation. Mr. de Valentin rose to his feet.

"My friends," he said, "Mr. Van Reinberg in his very plain words has put before you the outline of my plans. It is not very much more that I can tell you beyond this. The army and the navy are loyalists. I have friends everywhere. They wait only for an opportunity. When it comes, all will be easily arranged. Those who are indifferent I bribe. There is already a great secret society in both services. One whole army corps is pledged to me. Look, then, this is what happens. A great Power"—Mr. de Valentin looked steadfastly at me—"a great Power one day makes a demonstration against France. It is a bolt from a clear blue sky; for my country, alas, is always preparing but never ready for war. The Press—I bribe the Press, those who are not already my friends—is hysterical. It strikes the note of fear, it attacks vehemently the government. The moment of war arrives. All is confusion. I appear! I address the people of France; I appeal to my fellow-countrymen. 'Put your trust in me,' I cry, 'and I will save you.' The Power of whom I have spoken stays its hand. Its Press declares for me. The government resigns. I march boldly into Paris at the head of the army, and behold—it is finished. The people are at my feet, the crown is on my head. Not a drop of blood has been spilt; but war is averted, and a great, new alliance is formed. France takes once more her place amongst the great nations of the world."

The man was in earnest beyond a doubt. The perspiration stood out in little beads upon his forehead, his dark eyes were on fire, his tone and manner tremulous with the eloquence of conviction. There was a little murmur from the women—a soft whisper of applause.

"Monsieur," I said quietly, "you have spoken well and convincingly. Pardon my presumption, if I venture to ask you one question. The Power of whom you have spoken—is it England?"

He faced me bravely enough.

"Sir," he said, "you ask a question which you know well it is impossible that I should answer. It is not for me to betray a confidence such as this. But to those who are curious, I would say this. Which is the Power, think you, most likely to play such a magnificent, such a generous part in the history of the nations? Answer your own question, Mr. Courage! It should not be an impossible task."

Six ladies leaned forward in their places, and looked at me with flashing eyes. It was a suitable triumph for Mr. de Valentin. And yet I knew now all that I desired. Dimly I began to understand the great plot, and all that it meant.

Mr. Van Reinberg looked across the table.

"Well, Stern?" he asked.

"My husband's cheque is ready," the lady at his side answered quickly. "I guess the Prince can have it right now, if he chooses."

"And mine!" five other ladies declared almost in a breath.

Mr. Van Reinberg smiled.

"Then I guess the deal is fixed," he remarked.

A dark-haired, little woman, sitting at my right hand, leaned forward towards Mr. de Valentin. She wore a magnificent crown of diamonds and sapphires, which had once

144

graced a Royal head, and a collar of diamonds which was famous throughout the world.

"I'd like to know," she said, "are we to choose our own titles? I've fixed on one I want."

Mr. de Valentin rose in his place.

"My dear lady," he said, "that would not be possible. To Mrs. Van Reinberg alone I have been able to offer the name she desired. That, I think, you will none of you object to, for it is through Mrs. Van Reinberg that you are all here to-night. For the rest, I have taken five of the great names of France, of whom to-day there are no direct descendants. It is for you yourselves to say how these shall be allotted."

Five ladies looked at one another a little doubtfully. Mr. Van Reinberg glanced at me, and there was a shrewd twinkle in his keen eyes.

"I should think you had better draw for them," he suggested. "Mr. de Valentin can write the names down on pieces of paper, and Mr. Courage, as a disinterested party, can hold the hat."

Mr. de Valentin shrugged his shoulders. His composure was not in the least disturbed. Whatever he may have felt, he treated the suggestion with perfect seriousness.

"If the ladies are agreeable," he declared, "I myself am quite indifferent how it is arranged. As regards the money, I shall give to each an undertaking to repay the amount in treasury notes within a year of my ascending the throne of my country."

My neighbor in the diamonds was still a little disturbed.

"Say," she inquired, "what do these titles amount to anyway? What shall we be able to call ourselves?"

"Either Madame la Comtesse or Madame la Marquise," Mr. de Valentin answered.

"Madame la Marquise!" she repeated, "that's the one I should like."

"So should I!" nearly all the ladies declared in unison.

Mr. Van Reinberg laughed softly to himself. For the first time, he seemed to be enjoying the situation.

"There's nothing for it but the hat, Mr. de Valentin," he declared.

Mr. de Valentin bowed.

"If every one is agreeable," he said stiffly, drawing a sheet of note paper towards him and beginning to write.

No one seemed quite satisfied; but, on the other hand, no one had any other suggestion to make. Mr. Van Reinberg leaned forward in his chair. He was beginning, apparently, to take a keen interest in the proceedings.

"Of course," he said softly, "the names could be read out, and if any of you took a special fancy to any of the titles, we could have a sort of auction, the proceeds to go to the fund."

Mr. de Valentin turned towards him with a stony look. Only his eyes expressed his anger.

"I presume that you are not in earnest, Mr. Van Reinberg," he said in a low tone. "Such a course is utterly out of the question."

Mr. Van Reinberg scratched his chin thoughtfully. Mr. de Valentin completed his task, and handed the slips of paper over to me.

"I shall ask Mr. Courage," he said, rising, "to distribute these through the agency of chance. For myself, I will, with your permission, retire. I will only say this to you, ladies, and to my friends. I hope and believe that it will not be long before I shall have the pleasure of meeting you under very different circumstances. You will be very welcome to the Court of France. I trust that together we may be able to revive some of her former glories, and I do believe that your presence amongst our ancient aristocracy will be for her lasting good."

So Mr. de Valentin left the room a little abruptly, and I thought it the most graceful thing he had done. I shook up the slips of paper, which he had given me in a hat, and handed them round.

There was an intense silence, and then a perfect babel of exclamations.

"Marquise de Lafoudrè! My, isn't that fine!"

"Comtesse de St. Estien! Well, I declare!"

"Comtesse de Vinoy. Say, Richard, are you listening? Madame la Comtesse de Vinoy. Great, isn't it!"

146

Mrs. Van Reinberg smiled upon them all the well-satisfied smile of one whose guerdon is deservedly greater than these. The little dark woman turned towards her abruptly.

"Tell us yours, Edith!" she exclaimed. "Don't say you're a Princess."

Mrs. Van Reinberg shook her head, unconsciously her manner was already a little changed. She was, after all, a swan amongst these geese!

"We are to have the Duchy of Annonay," she answered. "I suppose I shall be Madame la Duchesse."

Monsieur le Duc touched me on the shoulder.

"Here," he exclaimed in my ear, "let's get out of this!"

CHAPTER XXVII

INTERNATIONAL POLITICS

Mr. Van Reinberg led the way silently into the smoking-room, and ordered Scotch whisky. "Mr. Courage," he said from the depths of his easy-chair, "I've got to ask you a question. What do you think of us?"

I laughed outright.

"I think," I answered, "that you are a very good husband."

He lit a cigar and pushed the box towards me.

"I'm glad you put it like that," he said earnestly. "And yet I guess we're to blame. We've let our wives slip away from us. Only natural, I suppose. We have our battlefields and they must have theirs. We rule the money markets, and they aspire to rule in society. I don't know how to blame my wife, Mr. Courage, but I hope you'll believe me when I tell you this: I'd sooner chuck ten or twenty millions into the Atlantic than be mixed up with this affair."

"I believe you, Mr. Van Reinberg," I answered.

He drew a sigh of relief. I think that my assurance pleased him.

"Tell me now," he said; "you are a man of common sense. Is that fellow a crank, or is he going to pull this thing off?"

I hesitated.

"His scheme is ingenious enough," I said, "and I believe it is quite true that there are a great many people in France who would be glad to see the Monarchy revived. They are a people, too, whom it is easy to catch on the top of a wave of sentiment. But, so far as I can see, there are at least two things against him."

"I trust," Mr. Van Reinberg murmured, "that they are big enough."

"In the first place," I continued, "I doubt whether Mr. de Valentin is a sufficiently heroic figure to fire the imagination of the people. He does not seem to me to have the daring to carry a mob with him, and he will need that. And in the second place—"

"Well?"

I glanced around the room. We were absolutely alone, but I dropped my voice.

148

"Is this in confidence, Mr. Van Reinberg?" I asked.

"Sure!"

"I do not believe that the Power whose intervention he relies so much upon is England. I do not believe that my country would risk so much to gain so little. We are on excellent terms with France as it is. Secret negotiations with Mr. de Valentin would be unpardonable chicanery on our part, and I do not think that our ministers would lend themselves to it."

Mr. Van Reinberg nodded.

"Whom do you believe he referred to then?" he asked.

"Germany," I told him. "That is where I believe that he has made a fatal mistake. He will never make a successful bid for the sympathies of the French people, if he presents himself before them backed by their historic enemy. Of course, you must understand," I added, "that this is pure speculation on my part. I may be altogether wrong. One can only surmise."

"On the whole, then," Mr. Van Reinberg asked anxiously, "you would not back his chances?"

"I should not," I admitted.

For a man who had just invested two million dollars in those chances, Mr. Van Reinberg looked remarkably cheerful.

"I'm right down glad to hear you say that," he admitted. "I know nothing about things over in Europe myself, and my wife seemed so confident. It'll be a blow to her, I'm afraid, if it doesn't come off; but I fancy it'll be a bigger one to me if it does!"

"You do not fancy yourself, then, as Monsieur le Duc," I remarked smiling.

He looked at me in speechless scorn.

"Do I look like a duke?" he asked indignantly. "Besides, I'm an American citizen, an American born and bred, and I love my country," he added with a note of pride in his tone. "Paris, to me, means the Grand Hotel, the American bar, the telephone and an interpreter. Mrs. Van Reinberg will stay at the Ritz. I guess I sleep there and that's all. No! sir! When I'm through with business, I'm meaning to spend what I can of my dollars in the country where I made them, and not go capering about amongst a lot of people whose language I don't understand, and who wouldn't care ten cents about me anyway. Some people have a fancy to end their days up in the mountains, where they can hear the winds blow and the birds sing, and nothing else. I'm not quite that way myself. I hope I'll die with my window wide open, so that I can hear the ferry-boats in the river, and the Broadway cars, and the rattle of the elevated trains. That's the music that beats in my blood, Mr. Courage! and I guess I'll never be able to change the tune. Say, will you pass that bottle, sir? We'll drink once more, sir, and I'll give you a toast. May that last investment of mine go to smash! I drink to the French Republic!"

I pledged him and we set down our glasses hastily. We heard voices and the trailing of dresses in the corridor. In a moment they all came trooping in.

Mrs. Stern looked round the room eagerly.

"If he's gone to bed I'll never forgive him," she declared. "I'm just crazy to know whether there isn't some sort of old chateau belonging to the family, that Richard can buy and fix up. Have you seen Mr. de Valentin?" she asked us.

"He's gone upstairs, sure enough," Mr. Van Reinberg answered. "Give the poor man a rest till the morning. Where's the Marquis? Come and have a drink, Marquis!"

"Quit fooling," Mr. Stern declared testily. "Here's Esther saying I'll have to wear black satin knickerbockers and a sword!"

"Wear them in Wall Street," Mr. Van Reinberg declared, "and I'll stand you terrapin at the Waldorf. Come on, Count, and the rest of you noblemen. Let's toast one another."

Mrs. Van Reinberg motioned me to follow her into the billiard-room.

"Well!" she exclaimed, looking at me searchingly,

I could scarcely keep from smiling, but she was terribly in earnest.

"I want to know exactly," she said, "what you think of it all. I know my husband has been making fun of it. He does not understand. He never will."

"Mr. de Valentin's scheme is a good one," I said slowly, "but he has not told us everything. If you want my opinion—"

"Of course I do," she declared.

"Then I think," I continued, "that his success depends a good deal upon something which he did not tell us."

"What is it?" she asked, eagerly.

150

"It depends, I think," I said, "upon the Power which has agreed to back his claims. If that Power is England, as he tried to make us believe, he has a great chance. If it is Germany, I think that he will fail."

She frowned impatiently.

"You are prejudiced," she declared.

"Perhaps," I answered. "Still, I may be right, you know."

"Germany is infinitely more powerful," she objected. "If she mobilized an army on the frontier, and France found half her soldiers disaffected—"

"You forget," I interposed, "that there would be England to be reckoned with. England is bound to help France in the event of a German invasion."

She smiled confidently.

"I don't fancy," she remarked, "that England could help much."

I shrugged my shoulders.

"Perhaps not," I admitted; "yet I do not believe that German intervention will ever win for Mr. de Valentin the throne of France."

She changed the subject abruptly.

"Apart from this, let me ask you something else, Mr. Courage. Supposing the plot should succeed. How do you think it will be with us at the French Court? You know more about these things than we do. Shall we be accepted as the original holders of these titles would have been? Do you think that we shall have trouble with the French aristocrats?"

"I am afraid, Mrs. Van Reinberg," I answered, "that I am scarcely competent to answer such questions. Still, you must remember that your country-people have secured a firm footing in France, and it will be the King himself who will be your sponsor."

She raised her head. Her self-confidence seemed suddenly to have become re-established.

"You are right, Mr. Courage," she said. "It was absurd of me to have any doubts at all. And now let me ask you—if I may—a more personal question."

"By all means," I answered.

"What have you and Adèle been quarrelling about?"

I looked at her in some astonishment.

"I can assure you," I said, "that there has been nothing in the nature of a quarrel between Miss Van Hoyt and myself."

She raised her eyebrows.

"Then why," she asked, "has Adèle gone away at a moment's notice?"

"Gone away!" I repeated incredulously.

"Is it really possible that you did not know?" Mrs. Van Reinberg asked. "She left just as we went in to the meeting. Mr. Stern's automobile is taking her to the depot."

"I had not the slightest idea of it," I declared. "Do you mean that she is not coming back?"

"Not at present, at any rate," Mrs. Van Reinberg declared. "You mean to tell me, Mr. Courage, that you have not quarrelled, and you did not know that she was going?"

"I had no idea of it," I said, "and I am quite certain that we have not quarrelled."

Mrs. Van Reinberg looked as though she found my statement hard to believe.

"You had better go to your room," she suggested, "and see if there is not a note for you! She must have a reason for going. She would tell me nothing; but I took it for granted that you were connected with it."

"Not to my knowledge," I assured her. "If you will excuse me, I will go and see if she has left any message."

I hurried up to my room. There was a note upon my dressing-table. I tore it hastily open. A few lines only, hastily scribbled in pencil:—

"*Dear*!

"Everything is changed since the news I told you of this evening. We must separate at once, and keep apart. Remember you have only five days. If you remain in America longer than that, your life is not safe.

"For my sake, go home! For my sake, also, burn this directly you have read it."

CHAPTER XXVIII

DOUBLE DEALING

"What sort of a place is this, anyhow, Guest?" I asked him, looking round me with some curiosity. We were a long way from Fifth Avenue, and what I had always understood to be the centre of New York; but the bar in which we sat was quite equal to anything I had seen at the Waldorf-Astoria. The walls were panelled with dark oak, and hung with oil paintings. The bar itself was of polished walnut wood. All the appurtenances of the place, from the white linen clothes of the two servitors to the glass and silver upon the polished counter, were spotless and immaculate. In addition to the inevitable high stools, there were several little compartments screened off, after the fashion of the old-fashioned English coffee-room of the seventeenth century, and furnished with easy-chairs and lounges of the most luxurious description. In one of these we were now sitting.

"Better not ask me that," Guest answered dryly. "There are some places in New York of strange reputation, and this is one of them. Now go ahead!"

I told him everything. He was a good listener. He asked no questions, he understood everything. When I had finished, he smoked a cigarette through before he said a word. Then he stood up and gave me my hat.

"Come," he said, "we have a busy morning before us, and we must catch the German steamer for Hamburg this afternoon."

"Back to Europe?" I asked, as we left the place.

"Yes!"

"But won't that rather give us away?" I asked. "I came to go out West, you know."

"We must try and arrange that," Guest answered. "I'll explain as we go along."

We climbed an iron staircase, which came down to the pavement within a few yards of the bar, and took the elevated railway up town. We descended at 47th Street and, after a short walk, entered a tall building, from the hall of which several lifts were running. We took one of them and stopped at the eleventh floor. Exactly opposite to us was a door, on the frosted glass of which was painted in black letters:

"*Philip* H. *Magg,*
agent"

We opened the door and entered. A middle-aged man, dark and with Jewish features, was sitting writing at a desk. There was no one else in the room, which was quite a small one. He glanced at us both carelessly enough, and leaned back in his chair.

"Good morning, Mr. Magg!" Guest said.

"Good morning, gentlemen!" Mr. Magg answered.

"You do not by chance remember me, I suppose?" Guest said.

A faint smile parted the lips of the gentleman in the chair. He rather avoided looking at us, but seemed to be glancing through the letter which he had just been writing.

"I never forget a face—and I never remember one—unnecessarily," he answered. "It is the A B C of my profession. To-day I believe that it is Mr. Guest, and his friend Mr. Courage, whom I have the pleasure of greeting."

For once Guest's face lost its immovability of expression. Even his tone betrayed his admiration.

"Wonderful as ever, my dear sir!" he exclaimed.

"Not in the least," Mr. Magg replied. "I know of your presence here very simply. Yesterday I cabled my refusal to accept a commission on the other side."

"They sent to you?" Guest exclaimed in a low tone.

Mr. Magg nodded.

"A very unimportant affair," he answered. "Just a record of your movements, and to keep you shadowed until the French steamer is in next week. Unfortunately they forgot one of my unvarying rules—never to accept a commission against a quondam client."

"You are a great man, Magg!" my companion exclaimed.

"I guess not," the other answered simply. "What do you want with me?"

"Look at my friend," Guest said.

Mr. Magg looked at me, and though his inspection was brief enough, I felt that, for the rest of my life, I was a person known to Mr. Magg.

"Well?"

154

"He is going to Europe with me this afternoon—and he is also going West, a long way west, to shoot anything he can find on four legs."

Mr. Magg nodded.

"He has to be duplicated then!" he remarked.

"Precisely," Guest assented.

"I understand," Mr. Magg said. "Which Mr. Courage am I to provide?"

"The one who stays," Guest answered.

"It can be done, of course," Mr. Magg said. "Pardon me one instant."

He stooped down and fished up a kodak.

"A little more in the light, if you please, Mr. Courage. Thank you! That will do! Now side-face."

I was snap-shotted twice before I knew where I was. Then Mr. Magg drew a sheet of paper towards him, and began to make notes.

"You are staying?" he asked.

"Waldorf-Astoria," I answered.

"You will be prepared to leave practically the whole of your effects there, and take your chance of ever seeing them again."

"Certainly," I answered.

Mr. Magg nodded and turned towards my companion.

"The other parties," he remarked, "do not stick at trifles. What do they want from Mr. Courage?"

Guest was serious.

"Well," he said, "they probably give him credit for knowing more than is good for him."

Mr. Magg was thoughtful for a moment.

"It will cost you five thousand dollars," he said, "and another five for life insurance."

"Agreed!" Guest declared.

Mr. Magg made another note upon the sheet of paper in front of him. Then he turned to me.

"You must bring me," he said, "before you leave, the key of your room, the clothes you are now wearing, the keys of your trunks, and any information you deem it necessary for your successor to have. The French boat is due here on Wednesday. On Tuesday, Mr. Courage shall leave the Waldorf for the Rockies. You will excuse me now! I have another appointment."

We were out in the street again in a few moments. I was feeling a little bewildered.

"These things," I said, "are arranged pretty quickly over here."

Guest nodded.

"Mr. Magg," he said, "is known as well in Europe as in New York. There is no one else like him. He has been offered retainers from the Secret Service of every country in Europe, but he prefers to work on his own. He has over a hundred assistants, and yet you never meet a soul in his office...."

When we returned there in a couple of hours' time, I thought, for a moment, that I was looking into a mirror.

A man of my own height, complexion and general appearance was standing by the side of Magg's desk. The latter looked backwards and forwards rapidly from me to my double.

"Very fair," he remarked. "Eyebrows a little deeper, and you must note the walk, George. Now please step into the next room and change clothes with this gentleman, Mr. Courage."

I did as I was told. The next room I found was a most delightfully furnished sitting-room, with a chair-bedstead in the corner, and a dressing-room and bathroom opening out from it.

"You don't wear an eyeglass, Mr. Courage?" my companion asked.

I shook my head.

"No glasses of any sort."

"You have no peculiarity of speech? I have noticed your walk. I suppose you are right-handed? Have you any friends over here whom I should be likely to come across?"

"I should think it very improbable," I answered. "I have made out a list of all the people I have met in America, and the house in Lenox where I have been staying."

My companion nodded.

"At the Waldorf," he said, "your room, I understand, is 584? You haven't made any friends there?"

"I have scarcely spoken to a soul," I answered.

"And you have made no arrangements out West?"

"None whatever," I answered.

"It seems easy enough," he declared. "Go on talking, if you don't mind. Your voice needs a little study."

When we reappeared in the outer room, Mr. Magg eyed us for a moment sharply, and then nodded.

"Good-day, gentlemen!" he said. "Pleasant voyage!"

We found ourselves outside with exactly an hour to catch the boat.

"I must buy some things for the steamer," I declared.

"I have everything that you will want," Guest declared. "I have sent my luggage down to the boat myself. No need for a man who doesn't exist, you see, to take any special precautions. Besides, we are quite four miles away from the docks."

We drove down to the steamer.

"Where are our state-rooms?" I asked.

Guest smiled.

"I haven't engaged any yet," he answered. "Don't look so startled. I can arrange it directly we're off. I expect the sailing lists will be looked through pretty carefully."

On the stroke of the hour the captain's whistle sounded, and the gangways were drawn up. The engines began to throb, in a few minutes we were on our way down the harbor. I stayed on deck, watching the wonderful stream of shipping and the great statue of Liberty until dusk. Soon the lights began to flash out all around us, and our pace increased. America lay behind us, and with it all the wonderful tissue of strange happenings and emotions, which made my few days there seem like a grotesque dream.

CHAPTER XXIX

I CHANGE MY NATIONALITY

Guest had never lost his sense of humor. As we left the agent's office and walked down Wellington Street into the Strand, he studied for a few moments my personal appearance, and began to laugh softly.

"My friend," he said, "you are wonderful! After all, beauty is but skin deep! Hardross Courage, if I remember rightly, was rather a good-looking fellow. Who would have believed that ready-made clothes from Hamburg, glasses and a beard could work such a change?"

I looked down a little disconsolately at my baggy trousers and thick clumsy boots.

"It's all very well," I replied; "but you're not exactly a distinguished looking object yourself!"

Guest smiled.

"I admit it," he answered; "but you must remember that for ten years, since I was kicked out of the diplomatic service in fact, I have studied the art of disguising myself. You, on the contrary, when I first had the pleasure of meeting you, were a somewhat obvious person. Who would have thought that a fortnight on a German steamer and six weeks in Hamburg would have turned you out such a finished article?"

"It's these d——d clothes," I answered a little irritably.

"They are helpful, certainly," Guest admitted. "Come, let us go and have luncheon *chez nous*."

We turned northwards again towards Soho, and entered presently a small restaurant of foreign appearance. The outside, which had once been painted white, was now more than a little dingy. Greyish-colored muslin blinds were stretched across the front windows. Within, the smell of cooking was all-pervading. A short dark man, with black moustache and urbane smile, greeted us at the door, and led us to a table.

"Very good luncheon to-day, sirs," he declared in German. "Hans, *hors d'oeuvres* to the gentlemen."

We seated ourselves, arranged our napkins as Teutons, and ordered beer. Then Guest assumed a mysterious manner.

"Business good, eh?" he inquired.

"Always good," the head-waiter declared. "We have our regular customers. Always they come!"

Guest nodded two or three times.

"Heard anything about your new proprietor?" he asked.

"Not yet," the man answered. "The nephew of Mr. Muller, who died, lives in Switzerland. A friend of mine has gone over to see him. He will buy the good-will—all the place. It will go on as before."

Guest smiled meaningly at me, a smile which was meant to puzzle the waiter.

"But," he said, "supposing some one should step in before your friend? Supposing Mr. Muller's nephew should have put this place into the hands of an agent in London, and he should have sold it to some one else! Eh?"

For the first time, the man showed signs of genuine uneasiness. His smile suddenly disappeared. He looked at us anxiously.

"Mr. Muller's nephew would not do that," he declared. "It was always promised to my friend, if anything should happen to Mr. Muller."

Guest smiled cheerfully.

"Ah!" he said, "it is unfortunate for your friend, but he will be too late!"

"Too late!" the man exclaimed.

"Too late!" Guest declared. "I will tell you some news. I have taken over the lease of this restaurant! I have bought the good-will and effects. I have the papers in my pocket."

The man was struggling with a more than ordinary discomposure.

"You make a joke, sir!" he exclaimed. "The place does not pay well. It is a poor investment. No one would be in such a hurry to take it."

Guest was much concerned.

"A poor investment!" he exclaimed. "We shall see. I have been in America for many years, my nephew and I here, and I have made a little money. I have bought the place and it must pay!"

160

The expression on the man's face was indescribable. He seemed stricken dumb, as though by some unforeseen calamity. With a half-muttered apology, he left us, and a few moments later we saw him leave the place. Guest looked at me meaningly.

"We are right then," he murmured. "I felt sure that I could not be mistaken. This is the place they have made their headquarters. That fellow has gone out to fetch somebody. Soon we shall have some amusement."

In less than five minutes the waiter returned, and there followed him through the swing doors a man to whom he turned and pointed us out. This newcomer was of almost aggressively foreign appearance. He wore dark clothes, a soft slouch hat; his black moustaches were waxed and upturned. His complexion was very sallow, and he was in a perspiration, as though with hurrying. He came straight up to us, and bowed politely.

"Is it permitted," he asked in German, "that I seat myself at your table? There is a little conversation which I should much like to have with you!"

Both Guest and myself rose and returned his bow, and Guest pointed to a seat.

"With much pleasure, sir," he answered. "My name is Mayer, and this is my nephew Schmidt. We have just returned from America."

More bows. The newcomer was exceedingly polite.

"My name," he announced, "is Kauffman. I am resident in London."

"My nephew," Guest continued, "has lived in America since he was a boy, and he speaks more readily English!"

Mr. Kauffman nodded.

"To me," he replied in English, "it is of no consequence. I speak English most. I presume, from what Karl there has told me, that it is your intention to go into the restaurant business in this country."

"Exactly," Guest answered. "I have a little money, and my nephew there knows something of the business. The head-waiter told you, perhaps, that I have taken this place."

"He did," Mr. Kauffman answered. "It is for that reason that I hurried here. I want to give you good advice. I want you not to lose your money."

"Lose my money," Guest repeated anxiously. "No! no! I shall take good care of that. If the books spoke the truth, one does not lose money here! No! indeed. I want to make a little, and then put in my nephew as manager. Myself I should like to go home in a year or two."

Mr. Kauffman leaned across the table. He spread out his hands, with their tobacco-stained fingers. He was very much in earnest, and he wished us to realize it.

"Mr. Mayer, you will have no money to take back from this place," he declared slowly and emphatically. "On the contrary, you will lose what you have put in. What you saw in the books is all very well, but it proves nothing. Amongst a certain community this place has become a meeting-house. It was to see and talk with old Muller that they came. A social club used to meet here—there is a room out behind, as you know. If a stranger comes here, it will be broken up, his friends will all eat and drink elsewhere!"

"But the good-will," Guest declared, "I bought it! I have the receipt here! I have paid good money for it."

Mr. Kauffman struck the table with his open hand.

"Not worth the paper it is written on, sir!" he exclaimed. "You cannot force the old customers to come. A stranger will lose them all!"

"But what am I to do?" Guest asked uneasily. "If what you say is true, I am a ruined man."

"I will swear by the Kaiser that it is true," Mr. Kauffman declared. "Now, listen. I will tell you a way not to lose your money. I myself had meant to take over this place. It would have been mine before now, but I never dreamed that any one else would step in. I know all the customers, they are all my friends. I will take it over from you at what you paid for it. No! I will be generous. I will give you a small profit to make up for the time you have wasted."

Guest's expression changed. He beamed on the other and adopted a knowing air.

"Aha!" he said, "I begin to understand. It is a matter of business this. So you were thinking of taking this restaurant, eh?"

Kauffman nodded.

"For me it would be a different affair altogether," he said hastily. "I have explained that."

Guest still smiled.

162

"I think, Mr. Kauffman," he said, "that I have made a good bargain. I am very much obliged to you, but I think that I shall stick to it!"

Mr. Kauffman was silent for several moments. The expression upon his face was not amiable.

"I understand," he said at last. "You do not believe me. Yet every word that I have spoken to you is truth. If a stranger becomes proprietor of this restaurant, its business will be ruined."

"No! no!" Guest protested. "They will come once to see, and they will remain. The chef, the waiters, I keep them all. There will be no alterations. The social club of which you spoke—they can have their room! I am not inquisitive. I shall never interfere."

"Mr. Mayer," Kauffman said, "I will give you fifty pounds for your bargain!"

Guest shook his head.

"I shall not sell" he answered. "I want my nephew to learn the business, and I want to go home myself soon. I have no time to look out for another."

"One hundred!"

"I shall not sell," Guest repeated obstinately. "I am sorry if you are disappointed."

Mr. Kauffman rose slowly to his feet.

"You will be sorry before very long that you refused my offer," he remarked.

Guest shook his head.

"No!" he said, "I think not. The people will come where they can eat well and eat cheaply. They shall do both here."

Kauffman remained for a few more minutes at our table, but he did not return to the subject. After he had left us with a somewhat stiff bow, he went and talked earnestly with Karl, the little head-waiter. Then he slowly returned.

"Mr. Mayer," he said, "I'm going to make you a very rash offer. I will give you £200 profit on your bargain."

"I am not inclined to sell," Guest said. "One hundred, or two hundred, or five hundred won't tempt me now that my mind is made up."

Kauffman left the restaurant without a word. Guest called the waiter to him.

"Karl," he said, "do you wish to stay here as head-waiter?"

"Certainly, sir," the man answered, a little nervously. "I know most of the customers. But I fear they will not stay."

"We shall see," Guest answered. "I am not in a great hurry to make money. I want them to be satisfied, and I want my nephew to be learning the business. You shall do what you can to keep them, Karl, and it will mean money to you. Now about this club! They spend money these members, eh?"

"Not much," Karl answered dubiously.

"That is bad," Guest declared; "but they must spend more. We will give them good things cheap. What nights do they meet?"

"No one knows," Karl answered. "The room is always ready. They pay a small sum for it, and they come when they choose."

"H'm!" Guest remarked. "Doesn't sound very profitable. What do they do—sing, talk, or is it business?"

"I think," Karl answered slowly, "that it is business."

"Well, well!" Guest said, "we are not inquisitive—my nephew and I. Can one see the room?"

Karl shook his head.

"Not at present," he answered. "Mr. Kauffman has a key, but he is gone."

"Ah, well!" Guest remarked, "another time. The bill, Karl! For this morning I shall call myself a guest. This afternoon we will take possession—my nephew and I!"

CHAPTER XXX

The "Waiters' union"

Guest and I had taken small rooms not a hundred yards from the Café Suisse, as the restaurant was called. We made our way there immediately after we had settled with our friend Karl, and Guest locked the door of our tiny sitting-room behind us. He first of all walked round the room and felt the wall carefully. Then he seated himself in front of the table and motioned me to draw my chair up almost to his side.

"My young friend," he said, "we have now reached the most difficult part of our enterprise. For several days we have not spoken together confidentially. I have not even told you the little I was able to discover in Hamburg. Shall I go on?"

"Of course," I answered.

"Take off your gloves," Guest said. "You cannot wear them in the restaurant. Good! Now, first of all, have you seen the morning papers?"

"No!" I answered.

He produced one from his pocket, and, placing it before me, pointed to a paragraph.

"Read," he said, "your obituary notice."

This is what I read:

"Tragic death of an English gentleman in the rockies

"Yesterday, whilst Mr. Charles Urnans and a party of friends from New York were returning to their camp near Mount Phoenix, they came across the body of a man in a deserted gorge half-way down the mountain. He had apparently been shot through the heart by a rifle bullet, and must have been dead for some weeks. From papers and other belongings found in his possesion, the deceased gentleman appears to have been a Mr. Hardross Courage of England."

LATER

"The body found this morning by Mr. Charles Urnans of New York has been identified as that of Mr. Hardross Courage, the famous English cricketer and well-known sportsman. Mr. Courage is known to have left New York some months ago, for a hunting trip in the Rockies, and nothing has been heard of him for some time. No trace has been discovered of his guides, although his camp and outfit were found close at hand. As no money or valuables were discovered on the body of the deceased, it is feared that he has met with foul play."

I think that no man can read his own obituary notice without a shiver. For a moment I lost my nerve. I cursed the moment when I had met Guest, I felt an intense, sick hatred of my present occupation and everything connected with it. I felt myself guilty of this man's death. Guest listened to my incoherent words gravely. When I had finished he laid his hand upon nine.

"Gently, Courage," he said. "I knew that this must be a shock to you, but you must not lose your sense of proportion. Think of the men who have sacrificed their lives for just causes, remember that you and I to-day, and from to-day onward, can never be sure that each moment is not our last. Remember that we are working to save our country from ruin, to save Europe from a war in which not one life, but a hundred thousand might perish. Remember that you and I alone are struggling to frustrate the greatest, the most subtle, the most far-reaching plot which the mind of man ever conceived. That poor fellow who lies out on the Rockies with a bullet in his heart, is only a tiny link in the great chain: you or I may share his fate at any moment. Be a man, Courage. We have no time for sentiment."

"You are right," I answered. "Go on."

"We are now," Guest declared, "in this position. In Hamburg I discovered the meeting-place of the No. 1 Branch of the Waiters' Union, and the place itself is now under our control. In that room at the Café Suisse will be woven the final threads of the great scheme. How are we to get there? How are we to penetrate its secrets?"

"We must see the room first," I remarked.

"And then there is the question of ourselves," Guest continued. "We are both nominally dead men. But none the less, our friends leave little to chance. You may not have noticed it, but I knew very well that we were followed home to-day from the café. Every moment of ours will be spied upon. Is the change in our appearance sufficient?"

I looked at myself in the little gilt mirror over the mantel-piece. Perhaps because I looked, thinking of myself as I had been in the days before these strange happenings had come into my life, I answered his question promptly.

"I cannot believe," I said, "that any one would know me for Hardross Courage. I am perfectly certain, too, that I should not recognize in you to-day the Leslie Guest who—died at Saxby."

"I believe that you are right," Guest admitted. "At any rate, it is one of those matters which we must leave no chance. Only keep your identity always before you. At the Café Suisse we shall be watched every moment of the day. Remember that you are a German-American of humble birth. Remember that always."

I nodded.

"I am not an impulsive person," I answered. "I am used to think before I speak. I shall remember. But there is one thing I am afraid of, Guest. It must also have occurred to you. Now that the Café Suisse is in the hands of strangers, will not your friends change their meeting-place?"

"I think not," Guest answered slowly. "I know a little already about that room. It has a hidden exit, by way of the cellar, into a court, every house of which is occupied by foreigners. A surprise on either side would be exceedingly difficult. I do not think that our friends will be anxious to give up the place, unless their suspicions are aroused concerning us. You see their time is very close at hand now. This, at any rate, is another of the risks which we must run."

"Very well," I answered, "You see the time?"

Guest nodded.

"I am going to explain to you exactly," he said, "what you have to do."

"Right," I answered.

"The parcel on the sofa there," he said, "contains a second-hand suit of dress clothes. You will put them on, over them your old black overcoat which we bought at Hamburg, and your bowler hat. At four o'clock precisely you will call at the offices of the German Waiters' Union, at No. 13, Old Compton Street, and ask for Mr. Hirsch. Your name is Paul Schmidt. You were born in Offenbach, but went to America at the age of four. You were back in Germany for two years at the age of nineteen, and you have served your time at Mayence. You have come to England with an uncle, who has taken a small restaurant in Soho, and who proposes to engage you as head-waiter. You will be enrolled as a member of the Waiters' Union, as a matter of course; but when that has been arranged you write on a slip of paper these words, and pass them to Mr. Hirsch—'I, too, have a rifle'!"

I was beginning to get interested.

"'I, too, have a rifle,'" I repeated. "Yes! I can remember that; but I shall be talking like a poll-parrot for I shan't have the least idea what it means."

"You need not know much," Guest answered. "Those words are your passport into the No. 1 Branch of the Waiters' Union, whose committee, by the bye meet at the Café Suisse. If you are asked why you wish to join, you need only say because you are a German!"

"Right," I answered. "I'll get into the clothes."

Guest gave me a few more instructions while I was changing, and by four o'clock punctually I opened the swing door of No. 13, Old Compton Street. The place

167

consisted of a waiting-room, very bare and very dirty; a counter, behind which two or three clerks were very busy writing in ponderous, well-worn ledgers, and an inner door. I made my way towards one of the clerks, and inquired in my best German if I could see Mr. Hirsch.

The clerk—he was as weedy a looking youth as ever I had seen—pointed with ink-stained finger to the benches which lined the room.

"You wait your turn," he said, and waved me away.

I took my place behind at least a dozen boys and young men, whose avocation was unmistakable. Most of them were smoking either cigarettes or a pipe, and most of them were untidy and unhealthy looking. They took no notice of me, but sat watching the door to the inner room, which opened and shut with wonderful rapidity. Every time one of their number came out, another took his place. It came to my turn sooner than I could have believed possible.

I found myself in a small office, untidy, barely furnished, and thick with tobacco smoke. Its only occupant was a stout man, with flaxen hair and beard, and mild blue eyes. He was sitting in his shirt-sleeves, and smoking a very black cigar.

"Well?" he exclaimed, almost before I had crossed the threshold.

"My name is Paul Schmidt," I said, "and I should like to join the Waiters' Union."

"Born?"

"Offenbach!"

"Age?"

"Thirty!"

"Working?"

"Café Suisse!"

"Come from?"

"America!"

He tossed me a small handbook.

"Half-a-crown," he said; holding out his hand.

168

I gave it him. I was beginning to understand why I had not been kept very long waiting.

"Clear out!" he said. "No questions, please. The book tells you everything!"

I looked him in the face.

"I, too, have a rifle," I said boldly.

I found, then, that those blue eyes were not so mild as they seemed. His glance seemed to cut me through and through.

"You understand what you are saying?" he asked.

"Yes!" I answered. "I want to join the No. 1 Branch."

"Why?"

"Because I am a German," I answered.

"Who told you about it?"

"A waiter named Hans in the Manhattan Hotel, New York."

I lied with commendable promptitude.

"Have you served?" he asked.

"At Mayence, eleven years ago," I answered.

"Where did you say that you were working?" he asked.

"Café Suisse!" I said.

It seemed to me that he had been on the point of entering my name in a small ledger, which he had produced from one of the drawers by his side, but my answer apparently electrified him. His eyes literally held mine. He stared at me steadily for several moments.

"How long have you been there?" he asked. "I do not recognize you."

"I commence to-day," I said. "My uncle has just taken the café. He will make me his head-waiter."

"Has your uncle been in the business before?" he asked.

"He kept a saloon in Brooklyn," I answered.

"Made money at it?"

"Yes!"

"Were you with him?"

"No! I was at the Manhattan Hotel."

"Your uncle will not make a fortune at the Café Suisse," he remarked.

"I do not think," I answered, "that he will lose one."

"Does he know what you propose?"

I shook my head.

"The fatherland means little to him," I answered. "He has lived in America too long."

"You are willing to buy your own rifle?" he asked.

"I would rather not," I answered.

"We sell them for a trifle," he continued. "You would not mind ten shillings."

"I would rather pay nothing," I answered, "but I will pay ten shillings if I must."

He nodded.

"I cannot accept you myself," he said. "We know too little about you. You must attend before the committee to-night."

"Where?" I asked.

"At the Café Suisse," he answered. "We shall send for you! Till then!"

"Till then," I echoed, backing out of the room.

170

CHAPTER XXXI

IN THE ENEMY'S CAMP

That night I gravely perambulated the little café in my waiter's clothes, and endeavored to learn from Karl my new duties. There were a good many people dining there, but towards ten o'clock the place was almost empty. Just as the hour was striking, Mr. Kauffman, who had been dining with Mr. Hirsch, rose from his place, and with a key in his hand made his way towards the closed door.

He was followed by Mr. Hirsch and seven other men, all of whom had been dining at the long central table, which easily accommodated a dozen or more visitors. There was nothing at all remarkable about the nine men who shambled their way through the room. They did not in the least resemble conspirators. Hirsch, who was already smoking a huge pipe, touched me on the shoulder as he passed.

"We shall send for you presently," he declared. "Your case is coming before the committee."

I rushed towards the front door, and stood there for a few moments to get some fresh air, for the atmosphere of the room was heavy with the odors of countless dinners, and thick with tobacco smoke. I smoked half a cigarette hurriedly, and then returned. There were scarcely half a dozen guests now in the place. One of them, a stout middle-aged woman, who had been sitting at the long table, beckoned me to her. She had very dark eyes and a not unpleasant face; but she wore a hideous black sailor hat, and her clothes were clumsily designed, and flamboyant.

"Is it true," she asked, "that this restaurant has changed hands?"

"Quite true, madam," I answered.

"Are you the new proprietor?" she asked.

"I am his nephew," I told her. "He is not here this evening."

"Are you going to keep on the eighteen-penny dinner?" she asked.

"We are going to alter nothing," I assured her, "so long as our customers are satisfied."

She nodded, and eyed me more critically.

"You don't seem cut out for this sort of thing," she remarked.

"I hope I shall learn," I answered.

171

"Where is the proprietor?" she asked.

"He is not very well this evening," I told her. "He may be round later on."

"You do not talk like a German," she said, dropping into her own language.

"I have been in America nearly all my life," I answered in German. "I speak English more readily, perhaps, but the other soon returns."

"Get me the German papers, please," she said. "I expect my man will keep me waiting to-night."

I bowed and took the opportunity to escape. I sent the papers by one of the waiters. Madame was a little too anxious to cross-examine me. I began checking some counterfoils at the desk, but before I had been there five minutes the door of the inner room was opened, and Mr. Hirsch appeared upon the threshold. He caught my eye and beckoned to me solemnly. I crossed the room, ascended the steps, and found myself in what the waiters called the club-room. Mr. Hirsch carefully closed the door behind me.

The first thing that surprised me was, that although I had seen nine men ascend the three stairs and enter the room, there was now, besides myself and Hirsch, only one other person present. That other person was sitting at the head of the table, and he was of distinctly a different class from Hirsch and his friends. He was a young man, fair and well built, and as obviously a soldier as though he were wearing his uniform. His clothes were well cut, his hands shapely and white. Some instinct told me what to do. I stood to the salute, and I saw a glance of satisfaction pass between the two men.

"Your name is Paul Schmidt?" the man at the table asked me.

"Yes, sir!" I answered.

"You served at Mayence?"

"Yes, sir!"

"Under?"

"Colonel Hausman, sir, thirteenth regiment."

"You have your papers?"

I passed over the little packet which Guest had given me. My questioner studied them carefully, glancing up every now and then at me. Then he folded them up and laid them upon the table.

"You speak German with an English accent," he remarked, looking at me keenly.

"I have lived nearly all my life in America," I reminded him.

"You are sure," he said, "that you understand the significance of your request to join the No. 1 Branch of the Waiters' Union?"

"Quite sure, sir," I told him.

"Stand over there for a few minutes," he directed, pointing to the farthest corner of the room.

I obeyed, and he talked with Hirsch for several moments in an undertone. Then he turned once more to me.

"We shall accept you, Paul Schmidt," he said gravely. "You will come before the committee with us now."

I saluted, but said nothing. Hirsch pushed away the table, and, stooping down, touched what seemed to be a spring in the floor. A slight crack was instantly disclosed, which gradually widened until it disclosed a ladder. We descended, and found ourselves in a dry cellar, lit with electric lights. Seven men were sitting round a small table, in the farthest corner of the place. Their conversation was suspended as we appeared, and my interlocutor, leaving Hirsch and myself in the background, at once plunged into a discussion with them. I, too, should have followed him, but Hirsch laid his hand upon my arm.

"Wait a little," he whispered. "They will call us up."

"Who is he?" I asked, pointing to the tall military figure bending stiffly down at the table.

"Call him Captain X," Hirsch answered softly. "He does not care to be known here!"

"But how did he get into the room upstairs?" I asked. "I never saw him in the restaurant."

Hirsch smiled placidly.

"It is well," he said, "my young friend, that you do not ask too many questions!"

The man whom I was to call Captain X turned now and beckoned to me. I approached and stood at attention.

"I have accepted this man, Paul Schmidt, as a member of the No. 1 Branch of the Waiters' Union," he announced. "Paul Schmidt, listen attentively, and you will understand in outline what the responsibilities are that you have undertaken."

There was a short silence. The men at the table looked at me, and I looked at them. I was not in any way ill at ease, but I felt a terrible inclination to laugh. The whole affair seemed to me a little ludicrous. There was nothing in the appearance of these men or the surroundings in the least impressive. They had the air of being unintelligent middle-class tradesmen of peaceable disposition, who had just dined to their fullest capacity, and were enjoying a comfortable smoke together. They eyed me amicably, and several of them nodded in a friendly way. I was forced to say something, or I must have laughed outright.

"I should like to know," I said, "what is expected of me."

An exceedingly fat man, whom I had noticed as the companion of the lady upstairs in the sailor hat, beckoned me to stand before him.

"Paul Schmidt," he said, "listen to me! You are a German born?"

"Without doubt," I answered.

"The love of your fatherland is still in your heart?"

"Always!" I answered fervently.

"Also with all of us," he answered. "You have lived in America so long, that a few words of explanation may be necessary. So!"

Now this man's voice, unimpressive though his appearance was, seemed somehow to create a new atmosphere in the place. He spoke very slowly, and he spoke as a man speaks of the things which are sacred to him.

"It is within the last few years," he said, "that all true patriots have been forced to realize one great and very ugly truth. Our country is menaced by an unceasing and untiring enmity. Wherever we have turned, we have met with its influence; whatever schemes for legitimate expansion our Kaiser and his great counsellors may have framed have been checked, if not thwarted, by our sleepless and relentless foe. No longer can we, the great peace-loving nation of the world, conceal from ourselves the coming peril. England has declared herself our sworn enemy!"

A little murmur of assent came from the other men. I neither spoke nor moved.

"There is but one end possible," he continued slowly. "It is war! It must come soon! Its shadow is all the time darkening the land. So we, who have understood the signs, remind one another that the Power who strikes the first blow is the one who assures for herself the final success!"

Again he was forced to pause, for his breath was coming quickly. He lifted his long glass, and solemnly drained its contents. All the time, over its rim, his eyes held mine.

"So!" he exclaimed, setting it down with a little grunt of satisfaction. "It must be, then, Germany who strikes, Germany who strikes in self-defence. My young friend, there are in this country to-day 290,000 young countrymen of yours and mine who have served their time, and who can shoot. Shall these remain idle at such a time? No! We then have been at work. Clerks, tradesmen, waiters, and hairdressers each have their society, each have their work assigned to them. The forts which guard this great city may be impregnable from without, but from within—well, that is another matter. Listen! The exact spot where we shall attack is arranged, and plans of every fort which guard the Thames are in our hands. The signal will be—the visit of the British fleet to Kiel! Three days before, you will have your company assigned to you, and every possible particular. Yours it will be, and those of your comrades, to take a glorious part in the coming struggle! I drink with you, Paul Schmidt, and you, my friends, to that day!"

He took a drink, which he seemed sorely to need. If any enthusiasm was aroused by his speech to me, if that was really what it had been, it was manifested solely by the unanimity and thoroughness with which all glasses were drained. A tumbler of hock was passed to me, and I also emptied it. Captain X then addressed me.

"Paul Schmidt," he said, "you know now to what you are committed. You are content?"

"Absolutely," I answered. "Is it permitted, though, to ask a question?"

"Certainly, as long as it does not concern the details of our plans. These do not concern you. You have only to obey."

"I was wondering," I remarked, "about France!"

Captain X twirled his fair moustache.

"It is not for you," he said, "to concern yourself with politics. But since you have asked the question, I will answer it. The far-reaching wisdom of our minters has been exerted to secure the neutrality of England's new ally."

My ponderous friend handed a paper to me across the table.

"See," he said, "it is the order for your rifle, and your ticket of membership. Hirsch!"

Hirsch nodded and took me by the arm. A moment later I descended the three steps into the restaurant, which was now almost deserted.

CHAPTER XXXII

SIR GILBERT HAS A SURPRISE

At half-past ten the next morning, I rang the bell at the door of my cousin's flat and inquired for Sir Gilbert Hardross. It was an excellent testimonial to my altered appearance, that the man who answered the door, and whom I had known all my life, declined promptly to admit me.

"Sir Gilbert is just going out," he said. "He is too busy this morning to see any one."

I kept my foot in the door.

"He told me to come," I declared. "I cannot go away without seeing him."

"Then you can stay where you are," he declared, trying to close the door. "You can see him as he comes out."

I stepped by him quickly. He was a small man, but he seized me pluckily by the collar. Just then we heard a door open, and my cousin stepped out dressed for the street.

"What is the matter, Groves?" he asked sharply.

"This fellow has forced his way in, sir," the man answered. "He says that you told him to come."

My cousin stood drawing on his gloves, and eyed me superciliously.

"I think," he remarked, "that that is a mistake, isn't it? I am quite sure that I have never seen you before in my life!"

I felt inclined to smile, but the man was watching us.

"I have some business with you, sir," I said deferenially. "I am not begging, and I will not keep you longer than two minutes."

My cousin stepped back into the sitting-room. I followed him and took the liberty of closing the door after me. Then I took off my hat, drew myself up to my full height, and dropped the foreign accent which I had been at so much pains to acquire.

"Don't you know me, Gilbert?" I asked.

He started at the sound of my voice, and took a quick step towards me. I held out my hand.

"God in Heaven, it's Hardross!" he exclaimed.

I laughed as our hands met.

"I shall not bother about my disguise any longer," I remarked. "It is evidently better even than I had hoped."

He wrung my hand. I was delighted to see that there was nothing in his face but joy.

"Old chap!" he exclaimed, "I'm delighted. I can't say more. You've knocked me all of a heap. For Heaven's sake talk! I should like to be quite sure that I'm awake."

"You're awake all right," I answered, "as sure as I'm alive! How well you look in black, old man! I suppose it's for me?"

He nodded.

"How on earth," he exclaimed, "could the papers have made such a mistake?"

"They weren't so much to blame. A man was murdered in the Rockies who called himself Hardross Courage, and who was travelling with my traps. Only you see it wasn't I!"

"A man who called himself Hardross Courage," Gilbert repeated, bewildered. "It's an uncommon name."

"The men who killed him," I answered, "thought that they had killed me. It's a long story, Gilbert. I've come here to tell you a little of it, if you can spare the time."

"Time! Of course I can," he declared. "Wait one moment while I go to the telephone."

I checked him on the way to the door.

"Not a word of this to any one, Gilbert," I said. "Not even to Groves there!"

He nodded and hurried out of the room. When he returned, he had taken off his hat and overcoat. He drew up two easy-chairs and produced a box of cigars.

"Now then!" he exclaimed, "for the mysteries! By Jove, I'm glad to see you, Hardross! Light one of those—they're the old sort——and go ahead."

178

"You're not a nervous person, are you, Gilbert?" I asked quietly.

"I don't think so," he answered. "You've given my nerves a pretty good test just now, I think! Why do you ask?"

"Because I am going to tell you secrets," I answered, "and because there are men in the world, men in London close to us, who, if they knew, would kill us both on sight."

"I am not a coward, if that is what you mean," Gilbert answered. "You ought to know that. Go ahead."

I told him everything. When I had finished he sat staring at me like a man stupefied.

"I suppose," he said at last, looking from his extinct cigar into my face, "that I am not by any chance dreaming? It is you, my cousin Hardross, who has told me this amazing story."

"Every word of which is true," I answered firmly, and I knew at once that he believed me.

"Well," he said, after a short silence, "where do I come in?"

"You fill a most important place," I answered. "I want you to see Polloch for us."

He nodded.

"Am. I to tell him everything?"

"Everything," I answered. "We have our Secret Service, I suppose, the same as other countries. It ought to be easy enough for them to act on our information."

"Have you seen the papers this morning?" he asked suddenly.

"No!" I answered. "Is there any news?"

"Our Channel Squadron," he said, "has received a very courteous invitation to visit Kiel during its forthcoming cruise."

"They will go?" I exclaimed.

"They leave in three weeks' time."

"If they enter German waters," I said, "not one of them will ever return. The bay will be sown with mines. It is part of the Great Plot."

"Yesterday's paper," Gilbert continued, "remarked upon the warm reception of the Prince of Normandy at the Berlin Court!"

"Ah!" I ejaculated.

"And the *Daily Oracle*," Gilbert went on, "had a leading article upon the huge scale of the impending German manoeuvres. Three days ago, the Kaiser made a speech declaring that the white dove of peace was, after all, more glorious than the eagle of war!"

"That settles it," I declared. "Gilbert, can you see the Prime Minister this morning?"

"I can and I will," he answered.

"You must convince him," I declared. "All the proofs I can give you are here. There is an account of the meeting at the summer house of Mrs. Van Reinberg at Lenox, with the names of all who were present and particulars of what transpired. There is a copy of my admission into the Waiters' Union, with some significant notes."

"This is all?" he asked.

"All!" I repeated. "Isn't it sufficient?"

"Polloch is an Englishman," my cousin said slowly, "and you know what that means. He will need some convincing!"

"Then you must convince him," I declared. "I am risking my life over this business, Gilbert, and we can none of us tell which way the pendulum will swing. I know that Polloch is one of the old school of statesmen, and hates Secret Service work. If it were not for that, such a plot as this could never have been developed under his very nose. It is absolutely necessary, Gilbert, that, under some pretext or another, the home fleet is mobilized within the next fortnight."

"It's a large order, Jim!"

"It's got to be," I answered. "You don't know what a relief it is, Gilbert, to sit here and talk to you about these things. Guest and I scarcely ever speak of them. And all the time the minutes slip by, and we get nearer the time. Guest and I are playing a desperate game after all—a single slip and we should be wiped out. And no one else knows."

Gilbert looked up at me quickly, as though a new thing had come into his mind.

180

"Jim," he said, "have you seen Miss Van Hoyt?"

"Not since I was at Lenox," I answered. "She must still believe that I was the man who was murdered in the Rocky Mountains—and I dare not let her know!"

"She certainly does believe it, Jim," my cousin answered gravely. "She was here last week—she is coming to see me again to-day."

"In England!" I exclaimed. "Adèle in England!"

"Not only that," my cousin continued, "but I believe that her coming was on your account."

"Tell me exactly what you mean," I demanded.

Gilbert leaned a little towards me.

"Jim," he said, "has there been anything between you and Miss Van Hoyt?"

"This much," I answered, "that but for these confounded happenings, she would have been my wife. If ever I do marry anybody, it will be she."

Gilbert nodded gravely.

"I thought so," he answered. "Well, I can tell you something that will perhaps surprise you. Miss Van Hoyt is also—"

He broke off in his sentence. We both sprang to our feet. A woman's clear musical voice was distinctly audible in the hall outside.

"It is she," he declared. "Do you want her to find you here, to know that you are alive?"

"Good God! No!" I answered.

He pointed to the curtains which separated the apartment from the dining-room. I stepped through them quickly, just as Groves knocked at the door.

CHAPTER XXXIII

A REUNION OF HEARTS

I heard the man's announcement, I was almost conscious of his surprise as he realized the fact that his master was alone. Then I heard Gilbert direct him to show the lady in; and a moment later my heart seemed to stand still. Adèle had entered the room. She was within a few feet of me. I heard the rustle of her gown, a faint perfume of violets reached me, and then the sharp yap of Nagaski, as Gilbert tried to include him in his welcome. Softly I stole a little closer to the curtain, and peered into the room.

Now I was never an emotional person, but there was a mist gathering before my eyes when at last I saw her. She was dressed in black, and her cheeks had lost all their color. There was a difference even in her tone. She spoke like a woman who has left the world of lighter things behind, and who has vowed her life to a single purpose. The impulse to rush out and take her into my arms was almost irresistible!

"I have come to see you, Sir Gilbert," she said, because I thought you would like to know something—of what I am going to do! you and—your cousin were great friends, were you not?"

"We were indeed," Gilbert answered.

"Then," she continued, "it may be some satisfaction for you to know that his death will not be altogether unavenged. I know more about it and the reason of it than you can know! I know that he was murdered, brutally murdered, because he had stumbled into the knowledge of some very extraordinary political secrets; and because, as an Englishman, he was striving to do what he believed to be his duty. His enemies were too many and too powerful! But what he began"—she leaned a little forward in her chair—"I mean to finish."

My cousin looked at her gravely.

"But will you not be running the same risk?" he asked.

Her lips parted in quiet scorn.

"A woman does not count the risks, when she has lost, through treachery, the man she cares for," she said quietly. "But for this, I should have been neutral. I am not an Englishwoman myself—in fact, I think my sympathies were with those who are working for her downfall. But everything is changed now! I am going to Paris to-night, and to-morrow I shall see the Minister of War and General Bertillet. One part of this great plot, at any rate, shall go awry."

182

"Tell me," my cousin asked, "what is—the Great Plot?"

The old habit was powerful with her. She looked nervously about the room.

"I cannot tell you," she answered, "only this! It is a wonderfully thought-out scheme, which, if it were carried out successfully, would mean the downfall of your country. The part of it which I know anything about is the part which secures the neutrality of France, and breaks up the alliance. I mean to prevent that."

"Take me into your confidence, Miss Van Hoyt," Gilbert begged.

She shook her head.

"You are wiser not to ask that" she said. "It is one of those cases where knowledge means death. But I can at least give you a hint. Have you any influence at all with any member of your government?"

"A little" Gilbert admitted.

"Then persuade them not to send your fleet to Kiel!"

Gilbert rose to his feet, and stood on the hearth-rug looking down at her.

"But, my dear young lady," he protested, "there are certain international laws which every nation respects. The game of war has its rules—unwritten, perhaps, but none the less binding. The visit of the English fleet to German waters is an affair of courtesy—"

She interrupted him ruthlessly.

"Did you ever hear of a warship called the *Maine*?" she asked scornfully. "Do you remember what happened to her? Can't you understand that these things can be arranged? Your better understanding with Germany hangs upon a thread. Germany knows exactly when to snap it. The English fleet will be allowed to leave Kiel harbor without a doubt, but every channel outside can be sown with mines in twenty-four hours. If I had proofs of what I know is being planned, I would give them to you! But I haven't. Go and do your best without them. The French ambassador may have something to say to your ministers in a few days which should open their eyes."

"I shall do my best," Gilbert said slowly, "but ours is an unsuspicious nation. I am afraid I shall be told that for Admiral Fisher to abandon his visit to Kiel now, without some very definite reason, would be impossible."

Adèle shrugged her shoulders.

"After all," she said, "it is your affair. England has no claims upon me. I have never lived here, I never shall—now! My work lies in France. Still, take my advice! Do what you can with your ministers."

She rose to her feet, and, in order to rearrange her scarf, which had fallen a little on one side, she set Nagaski on the ground. Very slowly, he made his way towards me, sniffing all the time. A few feet from the curtain he stopped. His hair stiffened. His little, beady eyes were like black diamonds. He barked angrily.

"Nagaski!" his mistress called.

He did not move. Neither dared I, for he was within a few feet of me. Adèle came across the room.

"Have you any secrets behind that curtain, Sir Gilbert?" she asked.

"A cat most likely," he answered nervously. "Let me pick him up for you."

Adèle stooped down, but he eluded her. With a low growl he sprang through the opening, and fastened his teeth in my trousers. Adèle turned to my cousin and her face was as pale as death.

"There was only one person in the world," she said, "to whom Nagaski used to behave like that. Sir Gilbert! what is there behind that curtain? I insist upon knowing. If there have been listeners to our conversation, it will cost me my life."

I stepped out. It seemed to me that concealment was no longer possible. She staged at me in bewilderment. I had forgotten my beard, my spectacles and shabby clothes. She did not recognize me!

"Has this person been here all the time? Is this a trap?" she demanded, turning to my cousin with flashing eyes.

I stepped forward.

"Adèle," I said, "don't you know me?"

She started violently. She looked steadily at me for a moment in dumb amazement. Her cheeks were ashen, her eyes dilated. And then recognition came—recognition in which there was also an element of terror.

"Jim!" she cried. "Jim! Oh! God!"

Her hands went to her throat. Her eyes seemed as though they would devour me. Yet she was not wholly sure! I took her into my arms!

184

"It was another man whom they shot, Adèle," I murmured. "It is I indeed, dearest."

But I spoke as one might speak to the dead. Adèle had fainted in my arms!

CHAPTER XXXIV

RIFLE PRACTICE

Adèle was herself in a very few minutes. My cousin considerately slipped out of the room. Directly she opened her eyes and found me kneeling by her side, her color became more natural.

"Jim," she murmured, "how did you do it? Tell me how it is that you are alive."

"A very simple matter," I answered. "I learned at Lenox all that I came to America to find out. I wanted to return to England without creating suspicion, so I hired a substitute to continue my trip."

"And he was killed?" she exclaimed.

"Yes!" I answered. "I insured his life, and I presume he knew his risks. In any case, the life of one man was a small thing compared with—you know what."

She looked into my face, and there was wonder in her eyes.

"How you have changed, Jim," she whispered. "It is you, isn't it? I can scarcely believe it. Can the months really write their lines so deeply?"

"Months!" I answered. "I have passed into a different generation, Adèle. It seems to me that my memory stops at a night a few months ago, at the Hotel Français. The things which happened before that seem to have happened to a different man."

"Could you play cricket now—or shoot partridges?"

"God knows!" I answered. "This thing has swallowed me up. The only thing that I do know is that I must go on to the end."

She sighed.

"And what is to become of me?" she asked.

I touched her lips with mine—and all the passion and joy of another sort of life warmed my blood once more.

"Wait only a few months, dear," I answered confidently, "and I will teach you."

Hope and incredulity struggled together in her face.

186

"You believe," she exclaimed, "that you will succeed?"

"Why not?" I answered. "I am counted dead. Could you yourself recognize me?"

She shook her head doubtfully.

"Your face itself is so changed," she answered. "My poor Jim, you are a very different person from the good-looking boy whose life seemed to depend upon catching that ball at Lord's. I think that you must have suffered a great deal."

"I have bought experience and the knowledge of life," I said grimly, "and I suppose I have paid a pretty stiff price for it."

I hesitated.

"Are you strong enough, Adèle," I asked, "for another shock?"

"I have lost the capacity for surprise," she answered. "Try me!"

"The real name of the man who is passing as my uncle—is Leslie Guest!"

She scarcely justified her last assertion, for her eyes were full of wonder, and she drew a little away from me as though in fear.

"Leslie Guest! The man who died at Saxby!"

"He did not die," I answered. "It was a case of suspended animation. When I read his letter to me, and when I saw you in the morning, I believed him dead. So did all the others. It was in the middle of the next night that the nurse discovered that he was alive! We sent for the doctor, and by the next morning he was able to speak. It was then that we determined to make use of what had happened."

"I see," she murmured. "That is why you changed the place of burial."

I nodded.

"Guest planned the whole thing himself," I said. "It was easily arranged. The curious part of it all is that he seems to have got the poison out of his system entirely now!"

She looked at me a little breathlessly.

"You are really wonderful people, both of you," she said.

"We have been very fortunate," I answered.

"And why," she asked, "are you dressed like a somewhat seedy-looking foreigner?"

"I am the head-waiter at the Café Suisse," I answered.

"Where is that?"

"In Soho! Guest—my uncle—is the proprietor."

"Listen, Jim!" she said. "Do not tell me why you are there, or what you are doing. I suppose I ought to be working on the other side—but I shall not. What I was going to do for the sake of you dead, I shall do now for the sake of you living. You and I are allies!"

"Pour la vie!" I answered, kissing her fingers; "you see even Nagaski is becoming reconciled to me."

She smiled and patted his head.

"At any rate," she said, "but for him I should not have found you! I wonder—"

I answered her unspoken question.

"I should not have come out," I told her. "To tell you the truth, Adèle, I am a different man now from what I was half an hour ago. I had forgotten that I was still a live being, and that the world was, after all, a beautiful place. I think I had forgotten that there was such a person as Hardross Courage. The absorption of these days, when one has to remember, even with every tick of the clock, that the slightest carelessness, the slightest slip, means certain death—well, it lays hold of you. No wonder the lines are there, dear!"

"Some day," she whispered, "I will smooth them all away for you! ..."

Gilbert came in a few minutes later.

"I am sorry to disturb you," he said, "but it is time I was off."

He glanced at Adèle.

"We have no secrets," I declared quickly.

He smiled.

188

"Well," he said, "I have an appointment with the Foreign Secretary at three o'clock this afternoon. Where can I see you afterwards?"

I hesitated. That was rather a difficult question to answer.

"I don't want to come here too often," I answered. "Do you mind sitting up a little later than usual tonight?"

"Of course not," he answered gravely.

"Then let me come to your club about a quarter to one," I said. "You can see me in the strangers' room."

Adèle rose and gave me her hand.

"I too, must go," she said. "I may write to you here—if I do I shall address the envelope to Sir Gilbert. Good-bye!"

I kissed her fingers, and she drew away from me a little shyly. My cousin saw her to the door, and in less than half an hour I was in my shiny dress coat, on duty for luncheon at the Café Suisse.

There were the usual crowd of people there, but no one whom I recognized particularly, until the stout lady who had talked to me the night before came in. I showed her to a table, and she talked to me graciously in German. She had discarded her black sailor hat, and had the appearance of being dressed in her best clothes.

"You see to-day I am alone," she remarked, drawing off her gloves and revealing two large but well-shaped hands, the fingers of which were laden with rings.

"You must take good care of me—so! And I am hungry—very hungry!"

It was a table d'hôte luncheon for eighteen-pence, and she ate everything that was set before her, and frequently demanded second helpings. All the time she talked to me, sometimes in German, sometimes in broken English. She seemed quite uneasy when I was not all the time by her side.

"My good man," she told me, "has gone away for two—three days. I am lonely, so I eat more! Why do you smile, Herr Schmidt?"

I shook my head.

"I know what you think," she continued, her black eyes upraised to mine. "You think that after all I am not so very lonely. Perhaps you are right. My good man he is much older than I. Sometimes he is very tiresome."

I murmured my sympathy. Just at that moment, Guest entered and passed through to the little office, all smiles and bows—the typical restaurateur. Madame eyed him keenly.

"It is your uncle, the new proprietor, is it not?" she asked.

I nodded, and left her on the pretext of a summons from another table. Something in Guest's look had told me that he wished to speak to me. He was taking off his overcoat when I entered the office.

"Be careful of that woman," he whispered in my ear. "She is dangerous."

I nodded.

"She is Hirsch's wife," I remarked.

"She passes as such, I know," he answered. "I have come across her once or twice in my time. She is cleverer than she seems, and she is dangerous. Any news?"

"We have a fresh ally," I answered. "She goes to Paris this afternoon."

"Miss Van Hoyt?" he exclaimed.

"Yes!"

He glanced at a calendar.

"Good luck to her!" he answered. "We will talk later. Go back into the restaurant."

I obeyed him, and almost immediately Madame called me to her side.

"I have a message for you," she whispered in my ear.

"You are to be at Max Sonneberg's rifle gallery at four o'clock this afternoon."

"From your husband?" I asked.

"So! You will be there?"

"Certainly! Where is it?" I asked.

"18, Old Compton Street," she answered. "Afterwards—"

She hesitated. I stood before her in an attitude of respectful attention.

190

"You like to come and drink a glass of beer with me?" she asked. "I live close there."

She was smiling at me with placid amicability. I was a little taken aback and hesitated.

"You come," she whispered persuasively. "No. 36, over the tailor's shop. You will find it easily. Afterwards I come here to dine! So?"

I was on the horns of a dilemma, for while my acceptance of her invitation might land me in a somewhat embarrassing position, I was still anxious to know exactly what her reasons were for asking me. She leaned a little closer towards me. Her black eyes were very bright and sparkling.

"I expect you," she declared. "So!"

I bowed.

"Thank you very much," I said, "I will come!"

She paid her bill and departed. I opened the door for her myself, and she whispered something in my ear as she went out. Karl, who had been watching us curiously, came up to me a few moments later.

"You know who she is?" he asked.

"Hirsch's wife," I answered, nodding.

"You had better be careful," he said slowly. "Hirsch is not a safe man to play tricks with."

I told Guest what had passed. He agreed with me that it was an embarrassing position, but he was insistent that I should go.

"One cannot tell," he remarked. "Even the cleverest women have their interludes. I rather fancy, though, that this time the lady has something more in her mind."

At four o'clock I presented myself at the door of an entry at the address which had been given me. An untidy-looking girl pointed out to me some stairs, over which was a hand pointing downwards, and a notice—

"MAX SONNEBERG'S RIFLE RANGE."

191

I descended the stairs, and found myself in a sort of cellar with two tubelike arrangements, down one of which a young man was shooting. Mr. Sonneberg rose slowly from a chair and came towards me.

"Paul Schmidt, is it not?" he asked.

I nodded.

"I was told to come here at four o'clock," I said.

"Quite right. Now tell me, what is this?" he asked, taking from a seat near and placing in my hand a weapon, similar to the one with which the boy was shooting.

I handled it curiously.

"It is a service rifle, reduced size," I remarked.

He nodded.

"Let me see you load it!" he directed, pointing to a box of cartridges.

I obeyed him without hesitation. He pointed to the unoccupied tube.

"Shoot!" he directed.

The tube was an unusually long one, and the bull's-eye rather small, but I fired six shots, and each time the bell rang. Mr. Sonneberg made a note in a book which he had taken from his pocket.

"Very good," he declared, "You have passed first class. You shall have your rifle to-night, and cartridges. Keep them in a safe place, and—remember!"

He pressed a cigar upon me, and patted me on the back.

"There are some who come here," he declared, "and I find it very hard to believe that they have ever seen a rifle before. With you it is different. You will shoot straight, my young friend. A life for every cartridge, eh?"

"I was always fond of shooting!" I told him.

"Come again, my young friend," he said cordially, "and show some of these others how a young German should shoot! You do not need practice, but it does me good to see a man hold a rifle as you do! So!"

192

I left the shooting gallery with flying colors. I was not so sure of my next appointment.

CHAPTER XXXV

"HIRSCH'S WIFE"

Madame received me with a beaming smile. I found her apartment furnished in the typical German fashion. There were two heavy mirrors, a plush tablecloth, and chairs covered with stamped velvet. A canary was singing in a cage fashioned like a church, a model of a German village stood proudly upon the sideboard. One end of the room was hung with thick curtains. Madame herself had arranged her hair with a heavy black fringe, and pinned an enormous blue bow at the back of her neck.

"We will sit together here," she said, indicating the sofa, "and we will talk of England. But first you shall open the beer."

There were several bottles upon the sideboard, and a corkscrew. I poured Madame out a glass and then one for myself. Madame was already making room for me by her side, when an inspiration came to me.

"You will drink a health with me?" I asked.

She raised her glass. I assumed a profoundly sentimental air.

"It is to a little girl in Frankfort," I said sighing. "To meine liebe Elsie! Soon I shall return to marry her!"

Madame raised her glass.

"To Elsie!" she repeated, and drank very nearly the whole of its contents. Then she set the glass down and looked at it thoughtfully.

"So," she murmured, "you have in Frankfort a little girl?"

"Yes, Madame!" I answered.

My hostess became thoughtful for a few moments. I could not flatter myself that it was disappointment which had furrowed her brow. She had, however, the air of one who finds it necessary to readjust her plans. It was during those few moments that I noticed the bulge in the curtains, concerning which I was wise enough to hold my peace.

"You will marry her some day?" she inquired.

"As soon," I answered, "as I have saved enough money. My uncle offers me the chance now. It is for that that I came back from America."

She nodded.

"Money," she remarked, "is not easily made. It takes time."

"It is true," I agreed.

"And you are very anxious to be married! She is pretty, this little one?"

"I wish I had her picture, Madame," I answered with enthusiasm, "that I could show you. You would understand, then, that I am very anxious indeed to be married."

"But to save money!" she said slowly, "it takes time that, eh?"

I could not see for the life of me what she was driving at, but I assented sorrowfully. At any rate, I was holding my own.

"Herr Paul," she said, raising her black eyes to mine, "have you ever looked about you for a way to make money more quickly?"

"I have thought of it often," I admitted, "but I have not succeeded. One cannot do as these foolish English do—back horses in races they never see. Stocks and shares I do not understand. I can only work; and my uncle, though he promises much, pays little."

She nodded her head.

"And all this time," she murmured, "the poor little girl waits!"

"What can one do?" I murmured dejectedly. She motioned me to draw a little nearer to her. "Herr Paul," she said, "I think that I could show you a way to make money, a large sum of money quickly, if you had courage!"

"Ah!"

I drew a little closer to her. She nodded again several times.

"You are not a fool, Herr Paul!" she remarked.

"I am not very clever," I answered sorrowfully; "but I do not think that I am a fool!"

"You are a member of the No. 1 Branch of the Waiters' Union," she said slowly.

"There is no money in that," I answered. "They even want me to pay something for my own rifle!"

"And when the time comes," she said thoughtfully, "you will probably be shot!"

"At least," I said hopefully, "I will shoot a few English first. But it is true what you say, Madame."

She whispered in my ear.

"The English government," she said, "would give a great deal of money to the person who told them about that No. 1 Branch. It would be easily earned; eh?"

I would have risen to my feet, but she pulled me back.

"Do not be foolish, Herr Paul," she said. "What has your country done for you? When you are older and wiser, you will understand that there is only one hand worth playing for in the world, and that is your own. I hate all this talk about patriotism and the Fatherland. They are all very well for holiday times; but the first thing in the world, and the only thing, is money. I want it and so do you! Let us earn it together."

I rose slowly to my feet.

"Madame," I said, "permit me to leave. I shall try to forget what you have suggested. I love my little girl and I love money. But never that way!"

I think that Madame was a little surprised. She tried to pull me down again by her side, but I resisted.

"You are a very foolish young man," she said vigorously. "Sit still and listen to me! What would your sweetheart say if she knew that you were throwing away a chance of marrying her, perhaps next month? Who can tell?"

"Madame," I said, "if you say more, you say it at your own risk. So far as we have gone I will try to forget. But I would like you to understand that I am not an informer."

Her face darkened.

"You are afraid of running a little risk," she muttered—"a very small risk! Remember that it would be a fortune. With what I can tell you it would be a fortune for both of us, and no one need know that it was us."

I took up my hat.

"Madame," I said, "I am sorry that I came. I wish you good afternoon!"

196

I think that she had made up her mind, then, to waste no more time upon me, for with a shrug of the shoulders she rose to her feet. She smoothed her hair in front of the glass and patted her bow.

"I think, Herr Paul," she said, "that if it had not been for the little girl in Frankfort, we might have arranged this—eh?"

I shook my head.

"Never!" I answered. "But if it had not been for her—"

"Well?"

"Madame knows," I answered, bowing over her bejewelled fingers. "Auf wiedersehen!"

She let me go then, and glad enough I was to get away from the atmosphere of cheap scent and Madame's stealthy advances. I realized, of course, that the whole affair was a trap, bred of this woman's suspicions of me. Nevertheless, I scarcely dared to hope that they were finally allayed. I told Guest about my afternoon's adventure, and he treated it very seriously indeed.

"She is one of the most dangerous women we could possibly have to deal with," he told me. "I have known of her all my life. She was in Paris twelve years ago, and she has twice brought Germany and France to the brink of war. She trusts or mistrusts wholly by instinct, and I have heard her boast that she is never mistaken. You have scored this time; but she won't let you alone. She is a regular sleuth-hound."

"I am warned," I assured him. "I shall do all that I can to keep out of her way."

I left a little before closing time that night, and made my way, by a circuitous route, to my cousin's club. I was shown into the strangers' room, and Gilbert came to me in a few moments. His face told me at once that he had met with no success. He carefully closed the door, and came over to my side of the room.

"Jim," he said, "it's horrible, but I've failed completely to convince—our friend. I haven't even made the least impression upon him. He listened to all that I had to say with a very polite smile, and every now and then kept on taking out his watch. When I had finished, he thanked me very much, but gave me clearly to understand that he considered I had been made a fool of. I tried to persuade him to see you, but he declined point-blank. Shall I tell you his message to you?"

I nodded.

"He sent his compliments, and begged you not to neglect your winter practice. Said he had set his heart upon the county winning the championship next season!"

"In plain words," I remarked bitterly, "he recommends me to mind my own business."

Gilbert nodded silently. He was unfolding an evening paper.

"It is like trying to save a drowning man, who persists in clinging to one's neck," I remarked. "Gilbert, I have had a German service-rifle given me to-day, with a plain hint that I may expect to be using it within a month. I even know which of the Tilbury forts I shall be expected to share in taking."

My cousin nodded and opened out his paper.

"The Channel Squadron," he announced, "leaves Devonport for Kiel on Thursday next. And here, in another part of the paper, is the little rift in the lute, Listen!—

"'We understand that a slight difficulty has arisen with Germany as to the proposed Morocco Commission. In view of the better understanding, however, now existing between the two governments, a speedy agreement is believed certain.'"

"We shall have an ultimatum," Gilbert declared grimly, "as soon as our ships are safely anchored in Kiel harbor. Polloch may change his tone then, but he will be a little too late. What can we do, Jim? Whom can we appeal to?"

"Heaven only knows!" I answered. "If Adèle succeeds in Paris, a hint may come from there."

"It is a slender reed," Gilbert said, "for so mighty an issue to rest upon."

I was thoughtful for a few moments.

"I have had proof within the last few hours," I said, "that I am under a certain amount of suspicion, and it is very possible that I am watched. Yet, after all, that is comparatively unimportant. Do you think that Polloch would see me?"

"I am sure that he would not," Gilbert answered promptly. "In fact, I may as well tell you at once, that he has set us down for a pair of cranks. He dismissed me to-day almost peremptorily. And I have reason to know that he has warned other members of the Cabinet against us. He told me plainly that it was the policy of his government to conciliate Germany, and he considered that a good deal of the ill-feeling in the past had been due to the fact that we were always over-suspicious of Germany and her actions. When I spoke of organized corps of waiters and clerks here, 300,000 of them, in commission, all of whom had had military training and possessed rifles, he practically called me an ass."

"Gilbert," I said slowly, "we are up against an *impasse*. I shall go back and consult with Guest. He is the most resourceful man I know. He may be able to suggest something."

Gilbert did not attempt to detain me. We walked together across the hall of the club, of which I, too, by the bye, was a member, and I was careful to carry my hat in my hand. Just as we were reaching the porter's box, a man in brilliant uniform, only partially concealed by a heavy military cloak, pushed open the swing doors and entered the club. He passed us by without a glance, but my heart was in my mouth.

"Gilbert," I whispered, "who was that?"

"Count Metterheim—he is on the military staff at the German Embassy. Why?"

I looked around. Count Metterheim had passed into the smoking-room, and there was no one else within ear-shot.

"He is also," I said, "on the committee of the No. 1 Branch of the Waiters' Union. I have been up before him at the Café Suisse!"

CHAPTER XXXVI

AN URGENT WARNING

Madame came alone to luncheon the next morning, and beckoned me to her table. "Well," she said, with her black eyes fixed steadily upon mine, "you are of the same mind, eh?"

I bowed.

"I prefer to think," I said, "that you were joking yesterday."

"So!" she answered, and began to eat. I gathered that I was dismissed. But presently she called me back again.

"You have many friends in London, Herr Paul?" she asked.

"None at all," I answered. "It is very lonely."

"I thought," she said, "that I saw you coming out of some flats in Dover Street the other day."

Madame was a little over-anxious. She was showing her hand too openly.

I leaned over the table, after a cautious glance around.

"I will tell you," I said, "since you are so kind as to be interested. I am looking for another situation. I think that I shall go into a private family."

"Another situation?" she exclaimed. "You are not satisfied here?"

I shook my head.

"My uncle," I said, "is a very mean man. He does not like to pay both Karl and myself—and he pays me very little. It is all promises!—and meanwhile Elsie waits."

Madame laughed, not altogether pleasantly.

"Elsie is likely to wait," she said. "You are too scrupulous, Herr Paul. I have shown you how to make a great deal of money."

"The money with which I marry Elsie," I answered, "shall not be blood money."

She let me go then, and I went away well pleased. I fancied that I was holding my own with Madame. And I had left the way clear for my next visit, which was no small thing.

At half-past three the restaurant was almost empty. Very soon after four I rang the bell of Lady Dennisford's town house in Park Lane. The man who opened it stared at my request to see her Ladyship. Eventually, however, I persuaded him to take in a message. I wrote a single word upon a plain card, and in five minutes I was shown into a small boudoir.

Lady Dennisford entered the room almost at the same instant from an opposite door. She was dressed in deep mourning; but it seemed to me that something of the old weariness was gone from her face. She looked at me searchingly, but obviously without recognition.

"I am Lady Dennisford," she said. "What is your business with me?"

I kept my eyes fixed upon her steadily.

"You do not recognize me, Lady Dennisford?" I asked.

She frowned slightly.

"Your voice is familiar," she answered, "and—why, you have a look of Hardross Courage! Who are you?"

"I am Hardross Courage," I answered. "Please do not look at me as though I were something uncanny. The report of my death was a little premature!"

She held out her hands.

"My dear Hardross!" she exclaimed. "You have taken my breath away! I am delighted, of course; but"—she continued, looking at me wonderingly—"what has happened to you? Where did you get those clothes?"

"I am going to explain everything to you, Lady Dennisford," I declared; "but before I do so, let me ask you something! I have given you one shock! Can you stand another?"

"What do you mean?" she asked.

"You see before you," I answered, "one dead man who has come to life. Can you bear to hear of another?"

Then every shred of color left her cheeks, and she trembled like one stricken with an ague. But all the time her eyes were pleading passionately with mine, as though it lay in my power to make the thing which she longed for true.

"Not—not Leslie! It is impossible."

"It is the truth," I answered. "He is alive."

I caught her just in time, and led her to the sofa. Her face was bloodless, even to the lips.

"Lady Dennisford," I said earnestly, "for his sake, for mine, bear up. Don't let me have to call for the servants. We are both in danger. Your people will probably be questioned."

"I will be brave," she answered with quivering lips; "but what did it mean—at Saxby then? Why, there was a funeral!"

"He was hard-pressed," I told her, "and it was the only way to save him. Be brave, Lady Dennisford, for I have come to you for help!"

"I will do everything you ask me to," she answered. "But tell me one thing more. He is alive!"

"He is in London," I answered. "He would have come himself, but the risk would have been greater. Will you listen to what I have to say?"

"Go on," she answered. "I am ready."

"You know what happened to him in Berlin fifteen years ago," I began. "He suffered for another's fault, but he suffered. His career was over, he was left with but two objects in life. One was a desire to reinstate himself; another, hatred for the country whose spies had brought ruin upon him. He changed his identity, but he remained at Berlin. For years he met with no success. Then fortune favored him. By chance he picked up one of the threads of the most cunning, the most cruel, the most skilfully thought-out plots against this country which the secret history of the world had ever known. He escaped to London, but spies were already on his track. I saved him from death once, and from that moment I, too, was drawn into the vortex. Let me tell you exactly what has happened to us since we joined forces."

Lady Dennisford was a good listener. I gave her, in as few words as possible, a faithful account of our adventures, and she never once interrupted me with a single question. When I had finished, she was perfectly calm and self-possessed.

"It is the most wonderful story I have ever heard," she declared with glowing eyes.

"The most wonderful part of it, from our point of view, is to come," I answered grimly. "We have a fair amount of proof, and we have laid all the facts before the Foreign Secretary and the Prime Minister."

"Well?"

"They absolutely refuse to believe us! Notwithstanding everything that we have put before them, the Channel Squadron has sailed for Kiel."

Lady Dennisford was a woman born for emergencies. She made no remark. She simply asked the one sensible question:

"What can I do?"

"Lord Esherville is your cousin, is he not?"

"Yes!"

"He is an influential member of the Cabinet. Will you go to him, tell him what you know of us, tell him who Guest is and his history? Try and convince him that we are not cranks, and that the country is really in the deadliest peril. Get him to see Polloch at once. Both Guest and myself are watched, because we have taken a café which is frequented by these people, but we will arrange a meeting, somehow. Try and get us a hearing."

She rose to her feet.

"When?"

"It must be within the next thirty-six hours," I answered, "or it will be too late."

"Where shall I let you know?"

"Letters are not safe," I answered. "I will call here at eleven o'clock to-morrow morning."

"You are not going," she exclaimed. "You will have some tea?"

I laughed outright.

"Please don't forget," I begged her, "that I have come about a situation. I am going to bring my references to-morrow."

"Absurd," she murmured softly. "Is—Leslie—also a—what did you say you were?—a waiter?"

"He is the proprietor of the Café Suisse in Old Compton Street," I answered. "I am his nephew learning the business."

"May I come and lunch?" she asked.

"I think not," I answered, smiling. "Our restaurant does not cater for such clients."

"Then how shall I let you know?" she asked.

"I will bring my references to-morrow," I answered—"at eleven o'clock."

I bought an evening paper on my way back to the Café Suisse. Of news here was very little. A leading article commented, with what to me seemed fatuous satisfaction, upon our improved foreign relations. Our *entente* with France was now in a fair way to be supplemented by a better understanding with Germany. Great things were hoped from the friendly visit of our fleet to Kiel; such international courtesies made always for good. And as I walked through the twilight with the paper clenched in my hand, I forgot where I was, I seemed to see over the grey sea to where, silently and secretly, the long service trains to Germany crawled to that far northward point, disgorging all the while their endless stream of soldiers, with mathematical regularity. The great plot moved. I read the extracts from the Berlin and Frankfort papers, and I knew that the wonderful example of the world's newest Power had been scrupulously followed. No word was there of secret manoeuvres amidst the wastes of those northern sands. I read the imposing list of battleships and cruisers, now ploughing their stately way across the dark waters, and I shuddered as I thought of the mine-sown track across which they would return. I remembered what a great German statesman had once boldly declared—"there is no treachery, if it be only on sufficiently great a scale, which success does not justify." And here was I, almost the only Englishman who knew the truth—powerless!

It was a busy night at the Café Suisse. Guest promenaded the room in his tightly fitting frock coat, his grey wig, and newly grown imperial, exchanging greetings with his clients in many languages. The long table was full! Hartwell was there, and Hirsch, and Kauffman, Madame and the others. And always I fancied that when I approached their table their voices dropped a little, and covert glances followed me when I turned away. Had Madame succeeded in making them suspicious, I wondered.

They went into the club-room as usual, and a quiet time followed in the restaurant. I went to talk with Madame, but she had little to say to me. Somehow, though, I could not move a yard without feeling that her eyes were upon me. Once only she beckoned to me.

"Well," she asked, "have you found the place yet, where you will make so much money that you can send for the beloved Elsie?"

204

I smiled deprecatingly.

"I have answered two advertisements," I said; "one at a club, but they were no good. I am going to see a rich English lady to-morrow morning. She may engage me as butler."

"You are a very foolish young man, Herr Paul," she said. "You do not know how to look after yourself. You will never make any money!"

It was one o'clock the next morning before Guest and I turned homeward to our rooms, for we had thought it well to separate, and I could tell him what had passed between Lady Dennisford and myself. He heard me without interruption, but I saw his face twitch with anxiety.

"It is almost the last chance," he muttered.

CHAPTER XXXVII

THE BLACK BAG

Lady Dennisford had failed. I saw it in her face as soon as I entered the room, and her first few words confirmed it.

"It's no use, Jim," she declared. "I've done my best, but there isn't a soul who will listen to me."

"Good God!" I murmured, and sat down on the sofa.

"There is not a single man in the Cabinet of the slightest influence," she continued, "who will take this affair seriously. Lord Esherville assured me solemnly that the whole affair was absurd and impossible. Polloch declares that we have been brought to the brink of war with Germany twice already, through treating her overtures with too much suspicion. He is absolutely determined that the mistake shall not be repeated."

"How about the massing of troops on the French frontier?" I asked.

"Ordinary manoeuvres," Lady Dennisford said. "The whole proceeding is absolutely open."

"And the reception of the Prince of Normandy by the Emperor?"

"An act of private courtesy. He ridicules the idea of German interference in French politics."

"And the rifle union?"

"If he believes in it at all, he looks upon it simply as a social and patriotic club, with which we have nothing to do. He ridicules the idea of regarding it as a force that could be utilized, even in the event of war."

"Then all three things happening together are merely coincidences?" I said bitterly. "He is blind enough to believe that?"

"He believes it most sincerely," Lady Dennisford answered.

"He will not stop the fleet going to Kiel?"

"He almost lost his temper at the bare suggestion," Lady Dennisford answered. "The slight hitch in the Morocco negotiations, he says, is simply owing to a misunderstanding, which will be cleared up in a day or two."

206

"Now I can understand," I said, "why, on the Continent, they always speak of British diplomacy with their tongues in their cheeks. To think that the destinies of a great country should be in the hands of men like this. Why, what can our Secret Service be about?"

"I believe," Lady Dennisford said, "that they have lately been presenting some disquieting reports. But it is all of no use. Every member of the Cabinet has got his back up. Lord Polloch says that Germany's friendship is absolutely necessary to us just now, and his Cabinet are determined to secure it."

"They will," I muttered, "at a price. Lady Dennisford, you will excuse me, I know. I must hurry back and see Guest."

"What is there left for you to do?"

"Heaven only knows!" I answered. "I am afraid we are at the end of our tether. If Guest has yet another card up his sleeve, he has kept it secret from me. I must see him at once."

"You will let me hear from you soon?" she begged as I departed.

"The newspapers may have more to tell you than I," I answered. "But I will come again—about the situation!"

Guest was waiting for me in the little glass enclosure we called an office. He saw my news written in my face.

"She has failed," he murmured.

"Utterly!" I answered.

We were both silent for a moment. The crisis of our fortunes had come, and, for the first time, I saw Guest falter. He removed his spectacles for a moment, and there was despair in his eyes.

"To think that we should have done so much—in vain," he muttered. "If one could think of it, there must be a way out."

His head drooped for a moment, and, glancing up, I saw Hirsch's dark inquisitive face watching us through the glass.

"Put on your spectacles and be careful," I whispered. "We are being watched."

Guest was himself again in a moment. I stepped out into the restaurant, where a few early luncheon guests were already arriving, and attended to my duties as well as I could. Hirsch and his wife were at their usual corner table, and they were presently joined by Marx, and two others of the committee before whom I had appeared. They all carried newspapers, and their conversation, though constant and animated, always languished at my approach—a fact which somewhat alarmed me. Madame watched me ceaselessly. I was perfectly certain once, when their heads were very close together, that I was the subject of their conversation. As soon as I realized this, I tried, without pointedly avoiding them, to keep out of their way.

We were very full that morning, and every one seemed to linger a long time over their luncheon. I was sick to death of the place, and my weary peregrinations from table to table, of the smile I wore, and the small jests and complaints I was forced to receive. The smell of the cooking was like some loathsome poison in my nostrils. I felt that morning, with the depression of despair upon my heart, that this was a fool's game which I had been playing. And then my heart stood still, and my recently developed powers of self-control received a severe shock. A familiar little yap had given me the first warning, I turned sharply round towards the door. Adèle, followed by a small elderly gentleman with a red ribbon in his buttonhole, had just entered.

I hastened towards them, and I addressed Adèle without a flicker of recognition in my face. I piloted them to a table a little apart, and handed her the carte.

"We shall remain," she said calmly, and with the air of one giving an order, "until the place is nearly empty. Come and talk to us as soon as you can safely."

I bowed, and handed them over to the waiter whose duty it was to serve at their table. As I passed down the room, I glanced towards the Hirsch table. They had ceased their conversation. Every one of them was staring at the newcomers. Soon they began to whisper together. Madame beckoned to me.

"Do you know who they are, Herr Paul, those people who have just come in?" she asked. "The little old gentleman, for instance! He is a Frenchman, is he not?"

I shook my head.

"They are strangers, Madame," I told her. "The gentleman has not spoken yet, but he wears a red ribbon in his coat."

Madame dismissed me with a little nod. I stood for a moment at a neighboring table, and I heard Hirsch's low voice.

"If it is he," he muttered, "there is mischief brewing, but he has come too late."

"If it is he," Madame murmured, "there is danger, there is always danger! You remember—at Brussels—"

I could hear no more, and I dared not show my curiosity. Somewhat abruptly, it seemed to me, the little party finished their luncheon and departed. The place began to grow emptier, I took careful stock of the few people that were left, and decided that the coast was clear. I returned to Adèle and her friend.

"Tell us both quickly," she said in a low tone, "exactly how things stand. This gentleman is the head of the French secret police. He is here to help, if it is possible."

"We have collected our material," I answered, "and placed it before the government here. We are up against an *impasse*. Through different sources we have approached several members of the Cabinet. The result has been the same in every case. We are treated as madmen. Polloch will do nothing. The fleet has sailed, the rifles remain in the alleys of Soho and Heaven knows where. Not a single precautionary measure has been taken."

"In a lesser degree," she said, "I, too, have failed. I have succeeded in getting the royalist officers removed from the frontier army, but with regard to the navy, they would do nothing. The French government declined to believe that England might need assistance. We shall get no aid from there."

The little old gentleman leaned over and addressed me.

"What is your next step?"

"We have none," I answered bluntly. "I have only spoken for a minute or two with Guest since we heard of our last failure. Shall I fetch him?"

Adèle nodded. I went for Guest, who was promenading the room with his hands behind him, casting every now and then a sharp glance in our direction.

"They wish to speak to you," said.

He nodded and walked by my side.

"Our friend," he said, "is admirably disguised, but I recognized him. It is Monsieur Bardow, the cleverest man in France."

The two men exchanged bows and smiles. A waiter was standing near.

"I insist, Monsieur," Monsieur Bardow said, "that you and your nephew here join me in a bottle of wine. We will drink luck to your new venture. No! you must seat yourself, you and your nephew also!"

The farce was well kept up till the wine had been fetched and the waiter dismissed. Then Monsieur Bardow, with the mild expression of one who is still exchanging compliments, began to talk.

"Mr. Guest," he said, "I know you, and I think that you know me. We are both up against a hard thing—officials, who won't believe what does sound a little, perhaps, like a fairy story. I have succeeded a little, you not at all. I consider that a disaster to England, however, would be a disaster also to my country. I am here, therefore, to see if I can be of service to you."

Adèle leaned over towards us.

"Monsieur Bardow," she said, "has already been to his ambassador here!"

"And Monsieur Lestrange, who is good enough to have complete confidence in me, went at once to Downing Street," Monsieur Bardow explained. "When he returned he was angry!"

Guest tapped on the table with his forefinger.

"We have submitted our proofs," he said, "and they have been received with derision. Your ambassador, Monsieur Bardow, has spoken for us—and in vain! In what different manner can we approach this wooden-headed government? You have come here with something to propose! What is it?"

Monsieur Bardow nodded assent. He opened his mouth to speak. Suddenly his expression changed. He pointed to the door. The words came from his lips with the crisp rapidity of a repeating rifle!

"Who is that man?" he demanded. "Look! quick!"

I was just in time to see Hirsch's figure disappearing through the swing doors.

"A man named Hirsch," I answered.

"Who is he?"

"One of the committee of the Union," I answered.

"He left something with a waiter. Call the waiter quickly," Monsieur Bardow demanded.

I obeyed at once. The waiter, a Swiss-German, hurried to our table.

"What did Mr. Hirsch want?" I asked.

210

"He said that he was coming back to dinner this evening, and he left a bag," the waiter replied.

"Bring the bag here at once!" Bardow ordered.

Already he had risen to his feet. Something of his excitement had become communicated to us. In obedience to a peremptory gesture from Guest, the waiter hurried off, and returned almost immediately carrying a small black bag. Bardow held it for a moment to his ear. We were all conscious of a faint purring noise. Nagaski began to whine. Monsieur Bardow laid the bag gently down upon the table.

"Out of the place for your lives!" he commanded in a tone of thunder. I took Adèle's arm, we all rushed for the door. We had barely reached it before the floor began to heave, the windows to fall in, and a report like thunder deafened us! We emerged into the street, wrapped in a thick cloud of curling smoke, with masonry and fragments of furniture falling all around us. But we emerged safely, though of the Café Suisse there was scarcely left one stone upon another.

CHAPTER XXXVIII

A LAST RESOURCE

From all sides a great crowd gathered, with almost inconceivable rapidity. We pushed our way through, and gained a side street in safety. Monsieur Bardow arrested the attention of a four-wheeled cab galloping towards the scene of the disaster, and motioned us to enter. We all crowded in, and Monsieur Bardow, who entered last, gave an address to the driver.

"My friends," he said, as he finally stepped in, "I am afraid that it was my presence which has brought this disaster upon your café. My disguise is good, but not good enough to deceive the cleverest rogues in Europe. Let us take up our conversation where it was interrupted."

Guest nodded.

"The café has served its turn," he declared. "I am glad it is gone, although it was a close shave for us. Monsieur Bardow, I believe that you have something to suggest. There is no time to lose!"

The little Frenchman nodded.

"I have," he admitted. "It is, perhaps, a forlorn hope, but it is our only chance. You have appealed to the government—you have failed! Appeal, then, to their masters."

"The people!" Guest exclaimed. "But how? There is no time!"

"There is only one way," Monsieur Bardow declared, "but it is a royal way. The things which we four in this cab know could be driven home to every living Englishman in little more than twelve hours' time, if we can only find—!"

"The Press!" I cried.

"If we can only find," Monsieur Bardow continued, with a little nod, "an editor man enough to throw the great dice!"

"Staunton!" Guest exclaimed.

"We are on our way there," Monsieur Bardow declared. "He is our one hope!"

I glanced towards Guest. There was a new fire in his eyes. I saw that the idea appealed to him. Nervously he flung down the window and let in the fresh air.

"A newspaper agitation," he muttered, "takes time, and if that destroyer does not leave by four o'clock to-morrow afternoon—"

Monsieur Bardow held up his hand.

"We go no further," he said. "It shall leave!"

The cab drew up before the palatial offices of the *Daily Oracle*. Monsieur Bardow took the lead, and with very little delay we were escorted to a lift, and into a waiting-room on the third floor. Here our guide left us, but only for a moment. In less than five minutes after we had entered the building we were in the presence of John Staunton, Editor and Managing Director of the *Daily Oracle*, a paper whose circulation was reported to be the largest which any English journal had ever attained. He was sitting, a slight, spare man, before a long table in the middle of a handsomely furnished room. Before him were telephones of various sorts, a mass of documents, and a dummy newspaper. He held out his hand to Monsieur Bardow, and half rose to his feet as he noticed Adèle.

"You have something to say to me, Monsieur Bardow?" he said rapidly. "As quickly as possible, if you please! This is the busiest hour of the day for me."

"You may reckon it, also," Monsieur Bardow said, "the greatest hour of your life, for I am going to give you an opportunity to-day of making history for all time."

Staunton raised his eyebrows. Yet it was easy to see that he was impressed.

"Your friends?" he asked, glancing towards us.

Monsieur Bardow turned to Guest.

"Forgive me," he said, "but it must be truth now, and nothing else. This is Lord Leslie Wendover, third son of the Duke of Mochester. You may remember Lord Leslie Wendover's name in connection with the Berlin scandals fifteen years ago. This," he added, turning to me, "is Hardross Courage. You have heard of him, no doubt. The lady is Miss Van Hoyt of America."

Mr. Staunton bowed to all of us.

"Well?" he said.

"Each one of us," Monsieur Bardow said, standing, a slim, calm figure at the end of the table, with his fingers resting upon its leather top, "has a story to tell you. The stories vary only from their point of view. The end of all is the same. It is this: unless the English government sends a fast destroyer to Kiel before four o'clock to-morrow afternoon, the Germans will command London before seven days have

213

passed. And to the best of my belief, Mr. Staunton, you are the only man who can save this country."

"I will hear the story in a moment," Staunton said calmly. "First! You have been to the government?"

"We have," Guest answered. "They decline to hear us, believe us, or receive us. They scoff at our facts and ignore our warnings."

"You have some proofs?"

"We have almost convincing ones," Guest answered. "A further one almost cost us our lives a few minutes ago! The restaurant where we were deliberating was blown up by a bomb, placed there by some one who suspected us."

"The name of the restaurant?" Staunton asked.

"The Café Suisse," I told him.

From his look of interest, I knew that he had heard something about the place.

"Well," he said, "let me hear the stories."

Guest told his first, I followed, Adèle told hers, and Monsieur Bardow rapidly filled in certain blanks. All the while Staunton listened in silence. He had opened an atlas, and studied it carefully with a cigarette in his mouth, whilst Monsieur Bardow was speaking. When he had heard everything we had to say, he pushed the atlas back and leaned over the table towards us.

"You ask me," he said slowly, "to publish this story to-morrow. With what object?"

"That the people of this great country," Monsieur Bardow answered quickly, "should at least have a chance to themselves arrest this horrible disaster. Let them rise up and insist that before four o'clock tomorrow that destroyer leaves Devonport, with orders to stop our fleet entering Kiel harbor. Let them insist upon a general mobilization of the fleet, and the breaking up of this traitorous Rifle Corps. Your ministers have failed you! It is by favor of the people that they rule! Let the people speak!"

The man at the table moved his position ever so slightly. His eyes were fixed downwards. He seemed to be thinking deeply. Monsieur Bardow continued.

"My friends here," he said, "have done all that can be done with members of the Cabinet, not only themselves, but in the person of others of great influence. The

214

appeal to you is practically an appeal to Caesar. Ministers are great, but you are greater. It is your hand to-day which grasps the levers which guide the world."

And still the man at the table was silent. Monsieur Bardow had more to say.

"I will tell you," he said, "what an American newspaper has done for us. To-morrow, at twelve o'clock, ten million of dollars is due to be paid to the agents of Prince Victor of Normandy, by the Credit Lyonnais of Paris. To-morrow morning, the *New York Herald*, in great type, exposes as a gigantic joke the whole affair! It will give the names of the American citizens, and the titles which their contribution to the Royalist cause in France is to secure. To-morrow, all New York will be convulsed with laughter—and I do not think that that ten million dollars will be cabled to the Credit Lyonnais."

The man at the table lifted his head. His face was the face of a man who had been in pain.

"The two cases," he said slowly, "are not identical. The *New York Herald* perpetrates a huge joke upon its readers. Whichever way that affair ends, the newspaper has little to lose! You ask me, on the other hand, to risk ruin!"

"I do!" Monsieur Bardow answered. "I came to you, I and my friends here, because, from the first, you have shown yourself the uncompromising foe of German diplomacy and aspirations. I give you the chance to justify yourself. I know what it is that you fear, you do not doubt our faith—your only fear is lest we may have been deceived. Is that not so?"

Staunton assented gravely.

"You are asking me a great deal," he said. "The *Daily Oracle* represents a million of capital, it represents the life work of myself and many dear comrades. You ask me to stake our prestige, our whole future, upon your story. You ask me to publicly flout the government which we have supported through thick and thin. You give me no time to consult my colleagues—I must decide at once, yes or no! This is no small matter. Monsieur Bardow!"

"It is a tragedy," Monsieur Bardow answered. "I tell you that the future history of your country, perhaps of Europe, rests upon your decision. Don't let any smaller issue weigh with you for a moment. Be thankful that you are the man whose name will live in history as the savior of his country."

"Do not be too sure even of that," Staunton said. "Polloch is an obstinate man, and I know as well as any one, perhaps, how set the Cabinet are upon this German *rapprochement*. Still—you have fastened the burden on my shoulders, and I will carry it."

215

"Thank God!" Monsieur Bardow exclaimed, leaning over and shaking hands with Staunton. "Have no fear, my friend! It is Heaven's truth which you will print."

"I believe it," Staunton answered quietly. "Several mysterious things have happened during the last few days, and late this afternoon, consols began to fall in a most extraordinary fashion. The side-winds have blown some curious information to us, even this last hour or so! Now, gentlemen, and Miss Van Hoyt," he continued in a suddenly altered tone, "I have to send for all my editors and break up the whole paper. I shall be here till daybreak and afterwards. One condition I have to make with you."

"Name it," Monsieur Bardow declared.

"You must not leave this building till the paper is out. At any moment we may require information from one of you! You shall be made as comfortable as possible! Do you agree?"

"Of course," we all answered. "In fact," Guest remarked, "I fancy this is the safest place for us for a few hours."

Staunton looked at us all a little curiously.

"I suppose," he remarked, "you know the risk you have been running?"

"Our friends have reminded us," I answered.

An attendant came in, and Staunton handed us over to him.

"Show this lady and these gentlemen into the strangers' room," he ordered. "See that they have food and wine, and anything they require."

We left at once. In the passage we passed a little crowd of hurrying journalists on their way to answer Staunton's summons. In every room the alarm bell had sounded, and the making-up of the paper was stopped!

CHAPTER XXXIX

WORKING *THE ORACLE*

We had food and wine, plenty of it, and very excellently served. The room in which we were imprisoned was more than comfortable—it was luxurious. There were couches and easy-chairs, magazines and shaded electric lights. Yet we could not rest for one moment. Adèle and I talked for an hour or so, and we had plenty to say, but in time the fever seized us too. The roar of the machinery below thrilled us through and through. It was the warning which, in a very few hours, would electrify the whole country, which was being whirled into type. I thought of Madame, and once I laughed.

Three times Guest was sent for to give some information, mainly with regard to earlier happenings in Berlin, before our fateful meeting at the Hotel Universal. At last my turn came. It was interesting to visit, if only for a moment, the room where Staunton himself was writing this story.

He was sitting at his table, his coat off, an unlighted cigarette in his mouth, an untasted cup of tea by his side. Two shorthand clerks sat opposite to him, a typist was hard at work a few yards away. Staunton called me over to him. His voice was hoarse and raspy, and there were drops of sweat upon his forehead.

"Is it true, Mr. Courage," he said, "that you are still believed here to be dead?"

"Certainly!" I answered. "I have not communicated even with my lawyers. My substitute's fate was enough to make me careful!"

"Does any one know on this side?"

"My cousin, Sir Gilbert Hardross. He is with us. He saw Polloch and tried all he could himself."

"Good!" Staunton declared. "One more question. You say that on the committee of the Rifle Club was a German officer. Do you know who he was?"

"I do," I answered. "I saw him at the club when I went to meet my cousin. His name is Count Metterheim, and he is on the military staff at the Embassy here."

"Better and better," Staunton grunted. "That's all, thank you!"

I went back to the room where the others were waiting. The few people whom I passed looked at me curiously. Already there were rumors flying about the place. In less than five minutes I was summoned again. Staunton looked up from his writing.

"The news has come through of the wrecking of the Café Suisse," he said. "So far your story is substantiated. A man and a woman are in custody. Their names are Hirsch!"

"He's a member of the committee!" I exclaimed. "I saw him bring in the bag. It was Madame, his wife, who distrusted me all the time."

"Do you think," he asked, "that you were followed here?"

"Very likely," I answered

Staunton turned to a tall, dark young man who stood by his side.

"Tell Mr. Courage what has happened," he said.

The secretary looked at me curiously.

"A man arrived about a quarter of an hour ago who insisted upon seeing Mr. Staunton. He hinted that he had an important revelation to make with regard to the Café Suisse outrage. He would not see any one else, and tried to force his way into the place. In the scuffle, a revolver fell out of his pocket, loaded in all six chambers."

"What have you done with him?" I asked.

"Handed him over to the police," the young man answered; "but I am afraid they would never get him to the station. Have you looked out of the window?"

"No!" I answered.

He shrugged his shoulders.

"Do so!" he suggested.

I crossed the room, and, drawing the blind aside carefully, looked out. The street was packed with people! Even as I stood there, I heard the crash of breaking glass below!

"What does it mean?" I asked, bewildered.

"Your Rifle Corps, I should think," Staunton said, without ceasing writing. "We closed the doors just in time. They will try to wreck the place."

"We have telephoned to Scotland Yard and the Horse Guards," the man who stood by my side said, "and we have forty policemen inside the place now! Good God!"

218

The sudden roar of an explosion split the air. The floor seemed to heave under our feet, and the windows fell in with a crash, letting in the cold night air. We could hear distinctly now the shrieks and groans from below. It seemed to me that the roadway was suddenly strewn with the bodies of prostrate men. I sprang back into the room, we all looked at one another in horror. I think that for my part I expected to see the walls close in upon us.

"A bomb," Staunton remarked calmly. "Listen!"

He leaned a little forward in his chair, his pen still in his hand, his attitude one of strained and nervous attention. By degrees the tension in his face relaxed.

"It goes!" he muttered. "Good!"

He bent once more over his work. I looked at the man by my side in bewilderment.

"What does he mean?" I asked.

"The engine! The machinery is not damaged!" was the prompt reply.

I wiped the sweat from my forehead. The silence in the room seemed almost unnatural, and behind it we could hear the dull, monotonous roar of the machinery, still doing its work. Once more I turned to the window, and as I did so I heard the sullen murmur of voices. A little way down the street a solid body of mounted police were forcing back the people.

I made my way back to the other room, almost knocked down in the passage by a man, half-dressed, tearing along with a bundle of wet proofs in his hand. Adèle was standing by the wrecked window-frame—there were no more windows anywhere in the building—and she turned to me with a little cry.

"Jim!" she exclaimed, "Look! Look!"

I saw the line of fire and the policemen's saddles emptying fast. The people were closing round the building. Guest stood frowning by our side.

"This is what comes," he said, "of making London the asylum for all the foreign scum of the earth. How goes it, Courage?"

"Staunton is still writing, and the machinery is untouched."

"For how long, I wonder," he muttered. "The police are going over like ninepins."

I looked below longingly, for my blood was up. It was no ordinary mob this. They were beginning to fire in volleys now, and leaders were springing up. As far as we could see there was a panorama of white faces. It was easy to understand what had happened. We had been followed, and our purpose guessed. Tomorrow's edition of the *Daily Oracle* was never meant to appear!

"The place will be at their mercy in another few minutes," Guest said gloomily. "Twenty-four hours ago who would have dared to predict a riot like this, in London of all places? Not all the police in Scotland Yard would be of any avail against this mob."

"They may stop the paper," I said; "but Staunton's word—and these events—should go for something with Polloch."

Guest looked at me and away out of the window. Adèle was behind us, and out of hearing.

"Do you suppose," he said in a low tone, "that Staunton or any of us are meant to leave this place alive? I am afraid our friends below know too well what they are doing."

The door opened, and Staunton himself appeared. He looked years older than the strong, debonair man to whom I had told my story a few hours ago, but in his face was none of the despair which I had feared. He was pale, and his eyes were shining with suppressed excitement, but he had by no means the air of a beaten man. He came over to where we were standing.

"It is finished," he said calmly. "I read your story in print."

"Magnificent," I murmured, "but look! Do you think that a single copy will ever leave this place?"

He stood looking downwards with darkening face. For several moments he was silent.

"Look at them!" he muttered. "At last! The tocsin has sounded, and the rats have come out of their holes! Half a million and more of scum eating their way into the entrails of this great city of ours. For years we have tried to make the government see the danger of it. It is our cursed British arrogance which has shut the ears and closed the eyes of the men who govern our destinies. Supposing your invasion should take place, who is going to keep them in check? The sack of London would be well on its way before ever a German soldier set foot upon our coast."

"The question for the moment," I remarked, "seems to be how long before the sack of this place takes place. Look, the police are falling back. The mob are closing in the street!"

Staunton was unmoved.

220

"The soldiers are on their way," he answered. "We received a message just now by the private wire. The other has been cut. Look! My God, they've brought the guns! There are some men at headquarters who are not fools."

We pressed close to the windows, and indeed it was a wonderful sight. From the far end of the street, where the police had retreated, men were flying in all directions. We caught a gleam of scarlet and a vision of grey horses. There was no parley. The dead bodies of the police in all directions, and the crack of the rifles, were sufficient. We saw the gleam of fire, and we heard the most terrible of all sounds—the quick spit-spit of the maxims. I drew Adèle away from the window.

"Don't look, dear," I said, for already the ranks of the mob were riven. We saw the upflung hands, we heard their death cries. Leaders leaped up, shouting orders, only to go down like ninepins as the line of fire reached them. There was no hope for them or any salvation save flight. Before our eyes we saw that great concourse melt away, like snow before the midday sun. Staunton drew a great breath of relief.

"In half an hour," he said, turning abruptly to Adèle, "I will present you with a copy of the *Daily Oracle*."

CHAPTER XL

The issue of the *Daily Oracle* which appeared on the following, or rather the same, morning electrified Europe. Nothing like it had been known in the memory of man. For one halfpenny, the city clerk, the millionaire, and the politician were alike treated to a sensation which, since the days of Caxton, has known no parallel. The whole of the front page of the paper was devoted to a leading article, printed in large type, and these questions were the text of what followed:

"1. Do the Government know that within eighty miles of Kiel are one hundred and eighty thousand troops, with guns and all the munitions of war, assembled there for the purpose of an immediate invasion of England, assembled partly in secrecy, and partly under the ridiculous pretexts of manoeuvres?

"2. Do the Government know that it is a skeleton fleet, the weedings of the German navy, which awaits our squadron in Kiel waters, and that the remainder of the German fleet, at its full strength and ready for action, is lying in hiding close at hand?

"3. That there exists in London, under the peaceful guise of a trade union, an army of nearly 200,000 Germans, who have passed their training, and that a complete scheme exists for arming and officering same at practically a moment's notice?

"4. That a German army is even now massed upon the French frontier, prepared to support the claims to the throne of France of Prince Victor of Normandy, and that a conspiracy has been discovered within the last forty-eight hours amongst the French army, to suffer an invasion of their country on this pretext?

"5. That an American paper is to-day publishing the names of some of her richest citizens, who are finding the money for French Royalist agents, to buy over the wavering officers of the army of our ally, the army of the French Republic!

"There is ignorance which is folly," the article went on, "and ignorance which is sin. The Government have proved themselves guilty of the first; if they show themselves guilty also of the second, the people of this country have the right to hurl from their places the fools who have brought them to the brink of disaster, and to save themselves. In their name, we demand two things:

"The dispatch of a gunboat with orders to the Channel Squadron to at once return to their waters.

"The mobilization of our Mediterranean Fleet."

With this text Staunton had written his article, and he had written it with a pen of fire. Every word burned its way home. With the daring of those few hours of inspiration, he had turned inference into fact, he had written as a man who sees face to face the things of which he writes. There could be but one result. At ten o'clock a Cabinet Council was called, and Staunton was telephoned for. Before midday, everything that he had suggested was done.

Even then, we knew that the question of peace or war must be trembling in the balance.

"Let it come if it will," Guest declared from his easy-chair in Gilbert's study, "the great plot is smashed. I pledge you my word that to-morrow the German newspapers will hold us up to scorn, will seek to make of us the laughing-stock of the world. They will explain everything. There will be no war. A German invasion of England is only possible by intrigues which will keep France apart, and treachery which will render our fleet ineffective. This plot has taken five years to develop, and I have been on its track from the first. Thank God, I can call myself square now with the past! ..."

There was no war, but the laughter of the German newspapers was a little hysterical. The Press of the world took the matter more seriously. But there was no war, and there are people even to-day, mostly his journalistic enemies, who say that Staunton was hoaxed.

* * * * *

"Do we receive our deserts in this world?" some one asked one night, when our dinner table at Saxby was like a suggestion of old times—and we all paused to think.

"Staunton has a peerage," Adèle remarked.

"Luckier than I," Guest laughed; only he called himself Guest no longer, but Lord Leslie Wendover. "My past disgrace had to be wiped out by an invitation to Windsor and a ribbon. Such are the ways of diplomacy, which never dare own a mistake."

"The amazing denseness of the man!" his wife murmured. "Do I count for nothing?"

He bent and touched her hand with his lips, as Adèle leaned forward and laughed at me across the table.

"I think," she said; "that you both deserve—what you got—us!"

Printed in Great Britain
by Amazon.co.uk, Ltd.,
Marston Gate.